Success in Business

Animer une réunion

Lisa Förster, Annette Joyce

Berlitz®

Contents

Sommaire

Introduction 5

Preparing a meeting 7

- Inviting people to a meeting 8
- Making meeting arrangements 11
- Rescheduling, cancelling or confirming a meeting 14
- Making the agenda 19
- Hands-on organisation 27

Arriving at the meeting 43

- Arriving in reception 44
- Introducing oneself and others 49
- Small talk 52
- Setting up the meeting room 57

Conducting a meeting 59

- Opening the meeting 60
- Guiding the discussion 64
- Bringing about a decision 70
- Closing the meeting 72

The meeting itself 77

- Roles at a meeting 78
- Active participation and asking for more information 80
- Expressing agreement and disagreement 87
- Making suggestions and having your say 98
- Enquiring and resolving misunderstandings 101
- Diplomacy and politeness 106
- What to do in case of language problems 113
- Voting 114

After the meeting 117

- Making the minutes 118
- Following up the meeting 124

Special types of meetings 127

- Meetings with customers 128
- Negotiations 132
- Briefing and brainstorming 141
- Jours fixes and kick-offs 145
- Telephone conferences 148

Literature 157

Index 159

Préface

Cet ouvrage est destiné à répondre aux interrogations de tous ceux qui sont amenés à développer des relations professionnelles avec des partenaires internationaux : tôt ou tard, vous devrez animer une réunion en anglais avec ces collaborateurs ou intervenir au cours de l'une d'elles. Est-ce déjà l'urgence dans laquelle vous vous trouvez aujourd'hui ou souhaitez-vous vous y préparer soigneusement pour un avenir proche ? Dans les deux cas, ce guide de la collection *Success in Business* de **Berlitz** répondra à vos attentes : les réunions professionnelles dans sa propre langue maternelle peuvent être difficiles et fastidieuses, aussi était-il nécessaire de proposer un guide permettant aux professionnels de mieux s'y préparer en anglais.

Cet ouvrage vous permettra ainsi d'acquérir : de nouvelles compétences linguistiques, un savoir-vivre professionnel et une aisance pour faire face à toutes les situations. Des formules de présentations au compte-rendu de réunion, en passant par les négociations, vous aurez ainsi tous les outils linguistiques et culturels en main.

Si votre pratique de la langue anglaise était jusque-là limitée, ce guide vous préparera à une entrée en scène réussie, sans crainte des faux-pas, du manque de vocabulaire et de confiance en soi. Pour ceux ayant davantage d'expérience, vous trouverez ici de nouvelles expressions et tournures très utiles qui viendront enrichir votre bagage linguistique. Pour être encore plus efficace, ce guide a été entièrement rédigé en anglais, afin que l'immersion dans la langue soit complète. Les enregistrements du vocabulaire disponibles *via* notre site Internet www.berlitzeditions.fr rendront son utilisation encore plus vivante et vous permettront d'améliorer votre prononciation.

Nous vous souhaitons tout le succès possible pour vos prochaines réunions en anglais !

Lisa Förster et Annette Joyce

Preparing a meeting

Préparer une réunion

Lors de la préparation d'une réunion, de nombreuses choses doivent être prises en compte, surtout si c'est vous qui êtes chargé de l'organisation. Réserver une salle de réunion n'est qu'une tâche parmi tant d'autres.

Dans ce chapitre, vous verrez comment :

- Convier les gens à une réunion (page 8) et réaliser les préparatifs (page 11).
- Déplacer, annuler ou confirmer une réunion (page 14).
- Procéder à l'ordre du jour (page 19).
- Organiser la réunion (page 27).

Inviting people to a meeting

Convier les gens à une réunion

In formal business relationships, you may wish to write a letter or email to a business associate to suggest an initial meeting. This correspondence can then be followed up with a telephone call or an email to confirm the meeting time and place.

Suggesting a meeting

Proposer une réunion

In an established business relationship, a less formal style can be adopted for suggesting meetings by both telephone and email. Email is especially useful if a number of participants are involved. In a formal email, the style of language, salutation and complimentary close is the same as that used in a letter.

to be *(was, been)* followed up with être suivi de

both à la fois, les deux

to be *(was, been)* involved être impliqué

a complimentary close une formule de politesse

Example: Formal UK-style letter / email

Modèle britannique de lettre / d'e-mail formels

Marketing proposal: initial meeting

Proposition marketing : réunion initiale

```
Dear Mr Smith

Thank you for your telephone call of this morning.
I am pleased to enclose [letter] / attach [email]
```

the information you requested and would welcome the opportunity to meet you in person to discuss the proposal and to answer any questions you may have.

I will contact you by telephone in the next few days to arrange a time that is convenient for you.

In the meantime, please do not hesitate to contact me if you require any further information.

Yours sincerely

David Dupont

Business Development Manager

to enclose sth *(with a letter)* joindre qqch *(à une lettre)*

to welcome the opportunity to ... être heureux de pouvoir...

to meet *(met, met)* s.o. in person rencontrer qqn en personne

to answer a question répondre à une question

to arrange a time convenir d'une heure

convenient pratique

in the meantime entre-temps

to require avoir besoin de

further informations des informations supplémentaires

Écrire les salutations et les formules finales convenablement

Dans les lettres et e-mails ***britanniques****, l'usage est d'omettre la ponctuation dans les salutations, dans les noms de personnes (***Mr, Mrs, Ms, Dr*** etc.) et dans les formules de politesse. Les lettres et e-mails se terminent par* ***Yours sincerely*** *quand le nom de la personne est cité, ou par* ***Yours faithfully*** *quand la lettre commence par* ***Dear Sir or Madam****. En anglais* ***américain****, un point (Am.* ***period****, Brit.* ***full stop****) suit les abréviations. Les salutations se terminent, quant à elles, par deux-points* ***(colon)****, sans espace (ex.* ***Dear Ms. Jones:****). Les formules de politesse standard sont* ***Sincerely yours****, et* ***Sincerely,****. Elles sont toutes deux suivies d'une virgule* ***(comma)****.*

Useful phrases

Less formal style

- I was wondering if we could meet in the near future to discuss …?
- Perhaps it would speed things up if we met face to face to discuss this?
- Shall we meet next week to discuss the details in person?

I was wondering if … je me demandais si…
to discuss sth discuter de qqch

it would speed things up if … les choses pourraient aller plus vite si…

Responding to a request for a meeting
Répondre à une invitation de réunion

Useful phrases

- I'm afraid my schedule is very full in the next few weeks. Would it be possible for us to discuss the matter by telephone instead?
- As we're both very busy, I would like to try to resolve the matter by telephone, if possible.
- I think it would be a good idea for us to meet.
- I agree that it would be beneficial for us to meet face to face.

I'm afraid … j'ai bien peur que…
a schedule un emploi du temps, un agenda
full chargé

to be *(was, been)* busy être occupé
to resolve the matter résoudre le problème

Making meeting arrangements
Les préparatifs de la réunion

In an informal setting, once you have agreed with your business partner that you would like to meet, arrangements can be made by telephone or email. In both cases, the language used for organising the meeting is informal yet polite.

an informal setting un cadre informel
once une fois que
to agree with être d'accord avec
yet pourtant

Who would like to meet when?
Qui souhaiteriez-vous rencontrer, et à quel moment ?

If you are organising a meeting with a larger number of participants and have to find out about their general availability on certain dates, 'Doodle' can help. This is a clever tool you'll find online free of charge at www.doodle.com. You create your doodle by just entering the dates and / or times you would like to suggest. A link to this doodle is automatically sent to your email account. You can then forward the link to all the prospective participants, asking them to state when they would be available and when not. There is also a field for comments.

to find *(found, found)* out about sth se renseigner sur qqch
availability la disponibilité
a clever tool un outil intelligent
free of charge gratuit
a link un lien (Internet)
to forward sth to s.o. envoyer qqch à qqn
prospective potentiel
to state indiquer

Lunch meetings

Déjeuners d'affaires

If you meet over lunch make sure you can still take notes on a small pad. Follow your host's lead with regard to drinking alcohol. In Great Britain, drinking alcohol in moderation is generally acceptable over lunch or dinner with business colleagues. However, if your business partners are sticking to water and you want to keep a clear head, avoid alcohol altogether.

a pad un bloc-notes
to follow sb's lead suivre l'exemple de qqn
with regard to en ce qui concerne
however cependant
to stick *(stuck, stuck)* to s'en tenir à, se contenter de
to keep *(kept, kept)* a clear head garder les idées claires
to avoid éviter
altogether totalement

Useful phrases

When?

Quand ?

- Would 20 November suit you?
- What does your schedule look like on 3 December?
- I'm afraid I'm away on business for the whole of that week. How about 25 November?
- What would be a convenient time for you?
- What time would suit you best?

to suit s.o. (best) convenir (le mieux) à qqn
to look like ressembler à, avoir l'air de
to be *(was, been)* away on business être absent pour affaires
the whole of the week toute la semaine

Where?

Où ?

- Where shall we meet? I would be happy to come to your office if that's more convenient.
- I can recommend a quiet restaurant near the city centre that would be easy for us both to reach.

To be confirmed (TBC)

À confirmer

- I need to check back with my colleague about that. Could I get back to you on that this afternoon?
- Could I confirm that with you tomorrow when I've spoken to my colleague?

It's a date

C'est d'accord

- Yes, that's fine. I look forward to seeing you at 3.00 p.m. on 25 November at your office.
- That's perfect for me, I can make it then. So let's fix our meeting for 25 November.

to check back with s.o. about sth vérifier qqch avec qqn

to get *(got, got* Brit. */ gotten* Am.*)* back to s.o. on sth revenir vers qqn à propos de qqch

to look forward to doing sth avoir hâte de faire qqch

I can make. Je peux venir.

to fix a meeting for caler une réunion à *(une date)*

Éviter les malentendus quant aux dates

En ***anglais britannique****, quand une date est exprimée en chiffres, le jour apparaît avant le mois. Par exemple, le 9 mars 2015* **(9 March 2015)** *devient* **09/03/15***. En revanche, aux*

> ***États-Unis**, la même date s'écrira* **March 9, 2015** *et deviendra donc* **03/09/15**. *Compte tenu de ces différences, il est préférable d'écrire les dates en toutes lettres.*

Useful grammar

The conditional tense, as in 'would' and 'could', is used frequently in the previous phrases. Conditional verbs make questions and suggestions sound open for discussion, rather than fixed and already decided, and therefore lend the suggestion a politer note.

rather than plutôt que
therefore donc, par conséquent

to lend *(lent, lent)* the suggestion a politer note conférer à la suggestion une note plus polie

Rescheduling, cancelling or confirming a meeting

Déplacer, annuler ou confirmer une réunion

In the interest of informing meeting participants as quickly as possible, it is common to postpone or cancel meetings by telephone or email, especially if this is necessary at short notice. In either case, it is a good idea to give the reason for changing the arrangement if appropriate, and to suggest another time for the meeting to take place.

as quickly as possible au plus vite
to postpone reporter
at short notice à la dernière minute

in either case dans les deux cas
to take *(took, taken)* place avoir lieu

Rescheduling a meeting

Déplacer une réunion

Examples

Example 1: Calling to reschedule a meeting

Appeler pour déplacer une réunion

A: Hello. This is Sarah from XYZ Com.

B: Oh, hi Sarah.

A: I'm calling regarding our meeting on 6 June at two o'clock. I'm afraid I have to ask if we could reschedule the meeting for the same time on 7 June? I'm very sorry to inconvenience you.

B: That's not a problem. Only, could we make it three o'clock on 7 June instead?

A: Yes, that's fine. Thank you for being so flexible. I look forward to seeing you at three o'clock on the 7th.

B: Okay, see you then. Bye bye!

A: Thanks again. Bye!

Example 2: Postponing a meeting by email

Reporter une réunion par e-mail

Subject: postponement of project meeting of 20 December

Dear Marc

Unfortunately it is necessary for me to change the arrangement we made for next Monday due to the rail strike that has been announced for next week. Please let me know what alternative day and time would be convenient for you.

```
I apologise for changing our arrangement at such
short notice and look forward to hearing from you
with regard to an alternative date and time.

Best regards

Simon
```

regarding concernant
due to en raison de
the rail strike la grève des chemins de fer

let me know ... indiquez-moi..., dites-moi...
an alternative day un autre jour
to apologise for doing sth s'excuser de faire qqch

Useful phrases

- I'm very sorry, but I'm afraid I have to postpone our meeting of next week, as I've been called to an urgent meeting at our head office. Would it be possible for us to meet the week after instead?
- I'm afraid I've been called away on urgent business next week, which unfortunately means that we have to reschedule the meeting we arranged for next Tuesday. Would any other days next week be convenient for you?
- I was wondering if it would be possible to bring the meeting forward by a week / postpone the meeting until the week after?

the head office le siège social
to be *(was, been)* called away on urgent business être appelé sur une affaire urgente

to mean *(meant, meant)* signifier
to bring *(brought, brought)* the meeting forward by a week avancer la réunion d'une semaine

Cancelling a meeting
Annuler une réunion

Useful phrases

- I'm very sorry, but I'm afraid it is necessary to cancel our meeting of next week until further notice.
- Due to unforeseen complications with the draft contract we are obliged to cancel next week's meeting.
- I very much regret to inform you that we have no other option but to cancel our meeting in Strasbourg on Friday.

until further notice jusqu'à nouvel ordre
unforeseen imprévu
the draft contract le projet de contrat

to have *(had, had)* no other option but to do sth ne pas avoir d'autre choix que de faire qqch

Confirming a meeting
Confirmer une réunion

It is a good idea to confirm an arrangement – especially one made by telephone – in writing. This also provides a good opportunity to give visitors travel directions if necessary.

When you write or email to confirm a meeting, it is recommended to send out travel directions and / or a map for reaching the meeting destination, so as to give your business partner plenty of time to make travel arrangements. See *Hands-on organisation* (p. 27) for tips on giving directions.

in writing par écrit

to send *(sent, sent)* out travel directions envoyer des indications relatives au trajet

a map un plan

plenty of time beaucoup de temps

tips des conseils

Examples

Example 1: Confirming a meeting by email

Confirmer une réunion par e-mail

Subject: marketing proposal meeting on 25 November

Dear Mr Smith

Following our telephone conversation of this afternoon, I am pleased to confirm our meeting at our offices on 25 November. The meeting is scheduled to take place from 3.00 p.m. to 4.30 p.m. Please find attached directions to our offices.

I very much look forward to meeting you on 25 November. Please do not hesitate to contact me if you require any further information in the meantime.

Yours sincerely

David Dupont

Example 2: Confirming a meeting (email to a colleague)

Confirmer une réunion (e-mail adressé à un collègue)

Subject: meeting of 25 March - Peter Smith ok

Sandra

Just to let you know that Peter Smith can make the meeting on 25 Nov after all. I made a reservation for the Arctic meeting room from 3 to 4.30. Hope you can still make it!

Best

David

following our telephone conversation... suite à notre entretien téléphonique

to hope espérer

Useful phrases

As a participant invited to a meeting, you can also confirm by phone:

- Hello. My name is Sarah Lejeune and I'm calling from XYZ Com. I am due to attend a meeting at your company on 14 May and I would just like to
  - – check the best way to reach your offices by car / public transport?
  - – confirm the time of the meeting.
  - – check whether there is an overhead projector in the meeting room?
  - – find out if there are any suitable hotels near to your offices?

a meeting room une salle de réunion

to attend a meeting assister à une réunion

to check vérifier

the best way to do sth le meilleur moyen de faire qqch

whether si

an overhead projector un rétroprojecteur

Making the agenda

Procéder à l'ordre du jour

All well-structured meetings should have an agenda, which is usually prepared by the chairperson. Depending on the type of meeting, agendas can be formal or informal, but all should start by stating the date, time and location of the meeting.

It is useful to include the name of the person who will be presenting a specific agenda item. You may also find it helpful to include a note of the time allocated to each point. Some more detailed agendas also state objectives for individual agenda items, for example: 'Agree on product design'.

Formal agendas differ from informal agendas in that they start with routine items, which always appear in a specific order. In addition, each point on the agenda is clearly numbered. Nowadays, agendas for all but the most important company meetings (board meetings, annual general meetings) tend to use an informal style.

the chairperson le président
to state the date fixer la date
the location of the meeting le lieu de la réunion
the items on the agenda les questions à l'ordre du jour
may *auxiliaire modal marquant la probabilité*
helpful utile
to allocate accorder, allouer
in addition de plus
each chaque
nowadays de nos jours
the board le conseil d'administration
an annual general meeting une assemblée générale ordinaire

Mots-clés et abréviations

Vous remarquerez que les ordres du jour, qu'ils soient formels ou informels, ont un style concis et ont tendance à s'écrire sous la forme d'une prise de notes, en omettant souvent les articles avant les noms et en utilisant des abréviations. Par exemple, **AOB** *signifie* **Any other business**, *« affaires diverses », ce qui renvoie à des sujets qui ne sont pas couverts par l'ordre du jour ou qui arrivent après la distribution de ce dernier.*

Examples

Example 1: Informal agenda (e.g. customer or team meetings)

Ordre du jour informel
(ex. réunions de clientèle ou d'équipe)

```
Agenda for end-of-year sales meeting
5 January, 9.00-10.30 a.m., Meeting room 2A
- Presentation of last year's sales figures
(Aurélie) - 15 mins
- Forecasts and targets for the coming year
  (Caroline) - 15 mins
- Analysis of last year's sales promotions (Marc) -
  15 mins
- Proposals for and scheduling of promotions for
  the current year (all) - 45 mins
```

Example 2: Formal agenda (e.g. board meetings)

Ordre du jour formel
(ex. réunions du comité de direction)

```
Agenda: Quarterly board meeting
10 April, 10.00-11.30 a.m., Board room suite
1. Apologies
2. Minutes of the last meeting
3. Matters arising from the minutes
4. Presentation of first quarter results (CEO)
5. Departmental presentations (heads)
6. Motions
7. AOB
```

end-of-year sales ventes de fin d'année

the sales figures les chiffres de ventes

a forecast une prévision

a target un objectif

quarterly trimestriel

minutes un compte-rendu

arising from résultant de

a motion une proposition

Compiling the agenda

Rédiger l'ordre du jour

Besides giving the meeting structure, the purpose of the agenda is to ensure that the time available is only used for discussing the items listed. Some people hold that topics that are important enough to be discussed should be included as items on the agenda, keeping AOB to a minimum. This can be done by asking participants to submit items for inclusion on the agenda. Email is a practical means of doing this, especially when a large group of people is involved. If the agenda is long, or in the case of a formal meeting, you may wish to circulate the draft agenda to participants as an email attachment, rather than including it in the body of an email.

Examples

Example 1: Asking for contributions to the agenda

Demander aux participants de contribuer à la mise en place de l'ordre du jour

Subject: agenda for end-of-year sales meeting, 5 January

Dear all,

Thank you all for agreeing to attend the end-of-year sales meeting on 5 January, from 9.00-10.30 a.m. in meeting room 2A.

As usual, the items below will be included on the agenda. Please could you let me know by 20 December if you would like any further items to be added to the agenda. I will then circulate the finalised agenda before the Christmas break.

- Presentation of last year's sales figures (Aurélie)
- Forecasts and targets for the coming year (Caroline)
- Analysis of last year's sales promotions (Marc)
- Proposals for / scheduling of promotions for the current year (all)

Regards,

Simon

Example 2: Circulating a draft agenda and asking for input

Faire circuler une ébauche de l'ordre du jour pour qu'il soit complété

Subject: draft agenda for quarterly board meeting, 1 April

Dear all,

Thank you for making time for the quarterly board meeting on 1 April, from 10.00-11.30 a.m. in the boardroom suite.

Please find attached a draft agenda for the meeting.

I would be grateful to receive any further submissions for the agenda by 25 March at the latest. Many thanks in advance.

Kind regards,

Simon Robert

the purpose le but	**below** ci-dessous
to ensure that s'assurer de / que	**to add** ajouter
a topic un thème	**a submission** une proposition
a means un moyen	

Submitting items for the agenda
Proposer des sujets à l'ordre du jour

If you wish to add an item to the agenda, make sure you submit it to the chair before the deadline for contributions. If this isn't possible – e.g. if an urgent issue has arisen after the deadline for submissions – let the chair know that you would like to include the item under 'Any other business'. Start your proposal by thanking the chair for the draft agenda and say why you think the item is relevant and should be included.

Useful phrases

- I would like to propose the item 'Potential overseas office' to follow item three, as this was discussed at the last managers' meeting and I think it is also relevant to the European sales team.
- I would like to insert the item 'Introduction of monthly sales targets' after item two, as this may be the last opportunity to discuss this issue prior to the sales conference next month.
- I recently received important new information from the customer regarding product specifications. If it is not possible to add the item to the agenda at this late stage, I would like to propose including it under AOB.
- I recently came across some software that could be of interest to the team. Since the deadline for submissions to the agenda has passed, I would like to put this item forward for inclusion under AOB.

the deadline le délai
an issue un problème
relevant pertinent
overseas à l'étranger
to arise *(arose, arisen)* survenir
prior to antérieur à
at this late stage à ce stade avancé
to come *(came, come)* across rencontrer par hasard, tomber sur
a software un logiciel

Circulating the agenda
Diffuser l'ordre du jour

After you have asked the participants for their contributions to the agenda, it is important to circulate the finalised agenda to them in good time. Email is an expedient way of doing this, but for important external meetings you may choose to send the agenda out by post instead, particularly if you have to enclose other important background documents with the original. This is also a good opportunity to ask participants what technical equipment they require for the meeting and if they have any special dietary requirements.

in good time à temps
expedient opportun
to send *(sent, sent)* sth out by post envoyer qqch par la poste
instead plutôt
background documents des documents annexes
special dietary requirements des particularités alimentaires

Example

Circulating the agenda

Diffuser l'ordre du jour

ABC SARL
26, av. Mounier
37000 Tours
France

Mr P Smith
Development Manager
EFG Co. Ltd
123 New Road
Newtown NEW 1IT
Great Britain

24 July 2010

Agenda for project meeting of 25 August

Dear Mr Smith

Thank you for your contribution to the agenda for the forthcoming project meeting. Please find enclosed a copy of the finalised agenda.

I also enclose a copy of the service agreement, signed by us, to be discussed under item four on the agenda.

I would be grateful if you would let me know by 10 August what technical facilities you will require for your presentation, and also whether you have any special dietary requirements we should note when arranging refreshments and lunch.

We look forward to seeing you on 25 August. In the meantime, please do not hesitate to contact me if you have any questions or require any further information.

Yours sincerely

Sylvie Martin, Project Manager

forthcoming prochain

facilities les installations, les équipements

Travel and weather tips

Conseils pour le trajet et la météo

If you didn't send out travel directions and / or a map for reaching the meeting destination when you confirmed the meeting (See *Confirming a meeting*, p. 17), you have another opportunity to do so when circulating the agenda. If your visitors are travelling from countries with different climates, they may also appreciate some tips on the weather and appropriate clothing for the time of year. For example: 'Please note that we are approaching the coldest time of year here in Scotland with frequent rainstorms and low temperatures. We recommend bringing warm and waterproof clothing for your visit.'

Hands-on organisation

L'organisation en pratique

Author Alan Barker *(How to manage meetings)* states: 'Ninety per cent of an effective meeting happens before it takes place.' Therefore, when organising the practical aspects of a meeting, it is essential to book everything in good time. Think ahead to what the participants might need – technical equipment, refreshments – and ask attendees about their requirements in advance when you confirm the meeting or circulate the agenda.

a rainstorm une pluie torrentielle
to book réserver

to think *(thought, thought)* ahead to penser avant tout à
the attendees les participants

Giving travel directions
Donner des indications sur le trajet

Providing your visitors with clear travel directions can save them considerable time when they come to arrange their trip. A good time to do this is when confirming the meeting or circulating the agenda, to give visitors plenty of time to make their travel arrangements.

Example

```
You can reach our office / the meeting venue as
follows:
By car:
Exit the M25 motorway at Junction 13
Follow the signs for Milton Keynes
At the first roundabout take the second exit to
Little Dunbary (follow A25)
Go straight on at the second roundabout
Turn right at the T-junction
Continue straight on until you reach the turning
for Little Dunbary Industrial Estate on your right
(opposite the Fox & Hounds pub)
You will find us at Unit 98, Road B. Entrance on
the left-hand side of the car park.
By public transport:
Nearest train station: Little Dunbary
Bus 42 to Little Dunbary Industrial Estate leaves
the bus station in front of the railway station
every 30 minutes (on the hour and half hour);
journey takes 30 minutes.
```

```
From Birmingham airport:
Take the airport shuttle to Birmingham city centre
bus station (shuttle leaves the bus stand in front
of the airport every 10 minutes); journey takes
40 minutes
Bus 42 to Little Dunbary Industrial Estate (see
above); journey takes 15 minutes
On arrival, please report to reception and we will
show you to the meeting room.
```

a motorway une autoroute
junction 13 la sortie n°13
to go *(went, gone)* straight on aller tout droit
a roundabout un rond-point
a T-junction une intersection en T
on the left-hand side sur le côté gauche
the nearest le plus proche
to leave *(left, left)* partir, quitter
a journey un trajet, un voyage
a shuttle une navette
above ci-dessus

Giving information on local accommodation

Informer sur les possibilités de logement

If visitors are travelling from far afield or from abroad, they may need to make an overnight stay close to the airport or to the meeting venue. You can save them much time and help them to arrange things by suggesting suitable places to stay in the area.

Useful phrases

- If you wish to make an overnight stay in the area, we can recommend
  - the Comfortable Inn, which offers reasonably priced accommodation and is located less than 500 metres from our office.

- the Travellers' Guest House, which is within walking distance of / a short bus / taxi ride from the office.
- the Luxus Hotel, which is a comfortable hotel located in the city centre and easily accessible from the office by taxi.
- the Wings Hotel, which is situated in the immediate vicinity of the airport and accessible by shuttle bus.

from far afield / abroad de loin / l'étranger
an overnight stay une nuitée
close to près de
the meeting venue le lieu de la réunion
to save s.o. much time faire gagner beaucoup de temps à qqn
in the area dans les environs
the vicinity les environs, le voisinage

Finding out about visitors' special dietary requirements

Se renseigner sur les particularités alimentaires des participants

If people from different cultures are attending the meeting, don't forget to bear their dietary requirements in mind when organising meals or refreshments. Some visitors may have food allergies that must be taken into consideration, so prior to the meeting it is a good idea to ask them to inform you of any special requirements when confirming the meeting or circulating the agenda.

Examples

Example 1: Asking about dietary requirements

Interroger les participants sur leurs éventuelles particularités alimentaires

Subject: project meeting of 25 August

Dear Mr Smith

Please find enclosed a copy of the agenda for the forthcoming project meeting.

As we will be organising lunch for the meeting attendees, I would be grateful if you would let me know by 10 August if you have any special dietary requirements we should note.

We look forward to seeing you on 25 August. In the meantime please do not hesitate to contact me if you have any questions or require any further information.

Yours sincerely

Sylvie Martin

Example 2: Communicating dietary requirements

Indiquer les particularités alimentaires des participants

Subject: project meeting of 25 August

Dear Ms Martin

Thank you for your letter of 24 July enclosing the agenda for the forthcoming project meeting.

Your letter requested information on special dietary requirements. I am allergic to wheat products and would therefore be most grateful if

```
you could make arrangements for gluten-free meals.
Many thanks in advance.
I very much look forward to seeing you at the
meeting on 25 August.
Yours sincerely
Peter Smith
```

Useful phrases

- I only eat halal meat / kosher food.
- I am a vegan / vegetarian.
- I don't consume any alcohol – even in cakes and sauces.
- Unfortunately, I'm allergic to gluten / wheat / dairy products / nuts / seafood.
- I have a wheat / dairy / nut / seafood allergy / lactose intolerance.
- I follow a gluten-free / wheat-free / dairy-free diet.
- I'm afraid I can't eat seafood.

to bear *(bore, borne)* sth in mind garder qqch à l'esprit

a vegan un végétarien

wheat le blé

gluten-free meals des repas sans gluten

the dairy products les produits laitiers

seafood des fruits de mer

Finding out about visitors' technical requirements

Se renseigner sur le matériel nécessaire aux participants

Many people bring laptop computers and other devices to meetings and there are a host of other types of equipment they might need you to supply. Don't forget to check in advance what the participants require. If you're responding to the organiser's request for information on technical equipment, make sure you reply before the deadline.

Useful phrases

- I would be grateful if you could let me know by 10 August what technical equipment you will need for the meeting / your presentation.
- Please let me know by 10 August if you require any technical equipment for the meeting / presentation.
- I would be most grateful if you could supply / provide an overhead projector and a local adapter for my laptop power cable.
- I will be bringing my laptop with me to the meeting. I would therefore be most grateful if you arrange for an extension lead to be provided.

a laptop (computer) un (ordinateur) portable
devices des dispositifs
to supply / to provide fournir

to let *(let, let)* s.o. know sth faire savoir qqch à qqn
a power cable un câble d'alimentation
an extension lead une rallonge

Booking meeting facilities
Réserver la salle et les équipements

Once you have gathered information on the participants' individual requirements and have a clear picture of what will be needed for the meeting, it's time to book the meeting room, necessary facilities and refreshments.

Examples

Example 1: Telephoning to book meeting facilities
Effectuer les réservations par téléphone

A: Hello, I'd like to book a meeting room for the Sales Department from 10.00 to 12.30 on 10 January, please.

B: Sure. How many people will be attending the meeting?

A: There'll be 15 of us.

B: Okay, I'll just check what's available ... Conference Room A is free at that time.

A: That's great. Could you just let me know how many power points are in that room?

B: I'll just check for you ... Room A has six power points.

A: Okay, in that case we'll need two extension leads with five sockets each, as most of the attendees will be bringing laptops.

B: That's fine. I'll reserve two extension leads for you.

A: Thank you. Could I also book an overhead projector?

B: Sure, no problem.

A: And some people will be joining us remotely. Could I book conference call equipment and a technician to set it up for us as well?

B: Certainly.

A: Thanks very much.

Example 2: Telephoning to arrange for refreshments
Commander les rafraîchissements par téléphone

B: Will you be requiring refreshments for the meeting?

A: Yes, please. We'll be taking a break at 11.00 a.m. Please could you arrange for refreshments for 15 people?

B: Certainly. Any special requirements?

A: Oh, yes. One person has a dairy allergy and has requested soya milk.

B: No problem at all. Do you need anything else?

A: The meeting will finish at lunchtime. Could you lay on some sandwiches for around 12.30, please?

B: Certainly. Any particular preferences?

A: Yes. We have two vegetarians and someone who only eats kosher food. Could you make provision for that, please?

B: Absolutely. Do you need anything else?

A: I think that's everything, thank you. If you could perhaps let your colleagues on reception know that some visitors from Japan will be joining us and to show them the way to conference room A?

B: Of course, we'll see to that.

to gather information rassembler des informations

power points / sockets des prises de courant

remotely à distance

to set *(set, set)* up installer

to lay *(laid, laid)* on prévoir

of course bien sûr

Intercultural considerations

Tenir compte des différences culturelles

Besides culture-related dietary requirements, other cultural aspects come into play when arranging a meeting involving participants from different parts of the world.

Times of the day and public holidays

L'heure et les jours fériés selon les pays

Particularly if you are organising a teleconference involving participants in different countries, it is important to ensure that the meeting will take place at a time that is reasonable for all the participants, wherever they are located. Remember, too, to check for important public holidays in your colleagues' countries. The website www.timeanddate.com contains a world clock and a meeting planner comparing times of the day in different countries. It also enables you to create calendars for different countries which display public holidays.

to enable s.o. to do sth permettre à qqn de faire qqch

to display montrer, présenter

Important time zones		
abbreviation	***explanation***	***where? when?***
Europe		
GMT (UTC)	Greenwich Mean Time (= Coordinated Universal Time)	Stays the same all year round; used all year round in Iceland and during the winter in UK and Ireland
DST	Daylight Saving Time (= Summer Time)	Term used when time is advanced by one hour during the summer time
BST	British Summer Time	UK, summer
IST	Irish Summer Time	Ireland, summer
WET / WEST	Western European Time / Western European Summer Time	
CET / CEST	Central European Time / Central European Summer Time	
EET / EEST	Eastern European Time / Eastern European Summer Time	
Canada and USA		
AST / ADT	Atlantic Standard Time / Atlantic Daylight Time	'Daylight Time' is used in summer time
EST / EDT	Eastern Standard Time / Eastern Daylight Time	
CST / CDT	Central Standard Time / Central Daylight Time	

Important time zones		
abbreviation	***explanation***	***where? when?***
MST / MDT	Mountain Standard Time / Mountain Daylight Time	
PST / PDT	Pacific Standard Time / Pacific Daylight Time	
Asia-Pacific		
CST	China Standard Time	Whole of China, all year round
IST	India Standard Time	Whole of India, all year round
JST	Japan Standard Time	Whole of Japan, all year round

The abbreviations 'a.m.' and 'p.m.' are often used in English: 'a.m.' stands for *ante meridiem* (= before noon / midday), 'p.m.' stands for *post meridiem* (= after noon / midday). 'Midday' (12.00 noon) is 12.00 p.m. (and therefore 13.00 = 1.00 p.m.) and 'midnight' (12.00 at night) is 12.00 a.m. (01.00 therefore = 1.00 a.m.).

Where confusion could arise, it is a good idea to use the 24-hour clock system for specifying times of the day (in which case you no longer need 'a.m.' or 'p.m.'), or to say, for example, 'seven o'clock in the morning' (meaning 7.00 a.m.) or 'seven o'clock in the evening' (meaning 7.00 p.m.).

Hierarchies and seating arrangements
La hiérarchie et le plan de table

However, in some countries, hierarchies play a more important role in business culture, so keep this in mind when making seating arrangements.

In general, the seat with the back to the door is the worst, as you cannot see who enters and leaves without turning around. The seats on both sides of the chair signal closeness to the leader. Seating arrangements must be carefully made in meetings with Asians: the top-ranking person should sit as closely as possible to the centre of the table with his or her subordinates on either side, in descending order of responsibility. The hosts should also sit closer to the door to greet the guests.

Asians usually bow as a greeting, with younger people and lower-ranking employees bowing lower to show their respect. An American-style slap on the shoulder would not be the right way of greeting a Japanese business partner and neither would the French *bise*.

to keep *(kept, kept)* sth in mind garder qqch à l'esprit

the closeness to le degré de proximité avec

top-ranking / low-ranking haut placé / de rang inférieur

to greet accueillir, saluer *(de manière générale)*

to bow saluer *(en s'inclinant)*

a slap on the shoulder une tape sur l'épaule

Peu importe l'âge
Dans les cultures anglophones, il est fréquent que les employés juniors participent aux réunions et que les cadres dirigeants les sollicitent quand leur domaine de compétences est concerné. Chaque personne, tous échelons hiérarchiques confondus, peut proposer des idées et poser des questions, même si elles ne sont pas en lien direct avec sa spécialité. Cela permet souvent de prendre du recul face au problème soulevé.

Evening entertainment

Les animations en soirée

Culture may also affect your choices of evening entertainment. Whereas dinner is universally accepted as the number one choice for the evening, the Japanese also take their business partners out to a Karaoke bar, and in England it is not unusual to attend a sporting event together or, in informal situations, to have a beer at the local pub.

Useful phrases

Inviting someone out

Inviter quelqu'un à sortir

- Can I invite you to join us for a drink before dinner?
- How about Joe's Karaoke bar for tonight?
- Our company sponsors the local cricket club. Would you like to join us for Saturday's match?

Accepting an invitation

Accepter une invitation

- What a brilliant idea! I'd love to join you.
- Absolutely! I've never been to a cricket match before, thank you!

- I'm afraid I'm tied up all Saturday with a family event.
- I'd rather stay in tonight. I am really tired from the long journey. I hope you understand.
- I'm afraid I'm not really into cricket.

an event un événement
to be *(was, been)* tied up être pris / occupé

not to be *(was, been)* really into sth ne pas beaucoup apprécier qqch

Arriving at the meeting

Arriver à la réunion

Le moment qui précède la réunion est un temps précieux qui permet de faire connaissance avec les différents participants. « Nous n'avons pas deux fois la chance de faire une bonne première impression », dit le dicton. C'est pourquoi se présenter et / ou faire les présentations sont des étapes très importantes. Enfin, l'environnement physique et l'équipement technique doivent aussi être installés et fonctionner correctement.

Dans ce chapitre, vous en saurez plus sur :

- L'accueil des visiteurs (page 44).
- Les présentations (page 49) et les conversations discours d'usage (page 52).
- La préparation de la salle (page 57).

Arriving in reception

Arriver à la réception

When arriving at reception, start by giving your name and the name of the person you are here to see.

Useful phrases

- Good morning, I'm here to see Ms Smith. My name is Sylvie Dupuis. I'm a little early, actually.
- Hello, my name is Sylvie Dupuis. I'm here for a meeting with / to meet Hilary Smith.

to be *(was, been)* a little early être un peu en avance
actually en fait

Être à l'heure

Alors que la ponctualité n'est pas toujours strictement observée lors des réunions internes dans les entreprises anglophones, elle est très importante lors des réunions extérieures. Le retard est considéré comme impoli, à moins qu'il ne soit justifié par de très bonnes raisons. Si votre retard est inévitable, prévenez la personne que vous allez rencontrer par téléphone en lui en faisant connaître la raison. Elle ne vous en tiendra pas rigueur si vous lui expliquez le problème et que vous la tenez informée.

Receiving visitors on arrival

Accueillir les visiteurs

If you are responsible for welcoming visitors, the reception you give them will form their first impression of the company. So it helps to have some friendly phrases at the ready. If your visitors are visiting the company for the first time, they may well have planned in extra time for their journey and arrived a little early. If there will be a short wait while the person they have come to see finishes what they are doing, put them at ease with a little small talk.

to be *(was, been)* responsible for être responsable de
to welcome accueillir
at the ready tout prêt
extra time plus de temps
while pendant que
to put *(put, put)* s.o. at ease mettre qqn à l'aise
to make *(made, made)* some small talk parler de choses et d'autres

Useful phrases

- Hello, Ms Dupuis. I'll let Hilary know you're here. Please take a seat for a moment.
- Good morning, Ms Dupuis. Welcome to ABC. Please take a seat. Ms Smith will be with you shortly.
- Ms Dupuis – Hilary knows you are here and her meeting is just coming to an end. She will be with you very shortly. Can I offer you something to drink while you wait?
- Ms Smith will be with you in just a moment. Can I bring you a tea or coffee in the meantime? Or some water?

to take *(took, taken)* a seat s'asseoir
shortly dans un court instant
to come *(came, come)* to an end toucher à sa fin
to wait attendre

Lift talk

Les banalités d'usage

Perhaps you've been asked to show the visitor in reception the way to the meeting room. On the way down the corridor or in the lift, it is customary for both parties to make some small talk to break the ice. In this situation, small talk is generally restricted to topics such as travel, or the weather.

to show *(showed, shown)* the way to montrer le chemin de

a corridor un couloir

a lift un ascenseur

customary habituel

the weather le temps, la météo

Example: arriving at a meeting and making lift talk

Arriver à une réunion et discuter de banalités

A: Ms Robinson? Good morning. I'm Marie Lejeune, Dr Baron's assistant. Welcome to Marseilles!

B: Thank you, Ms Lejeune. Nice to meet you!

A: Nice to meet you, too. Did you have a good trip?

B: Yes, thank you.

A: The meeting is on the second floor. Shall we take the lift or would you like to walk?

B: Actually, stretching my legs wouldn't be a bad idea, after so many hours on a plane! But before we go, is there a restroom I could use?

A: Of course, over there behind the column, to your left.

[Five minutes later]

B: So, that's better. Ready to roll.

A: Fine. Let's take the stairs. Is this your first time in Marseilles?

B: Yes, it is. I hope I'll have a chance to do a little sightseeing. I expect the harbour must be especially worth a visit?

A: That's right. It's really interesting. What was the weather like in New York when you left?

B: It was awful, really, slush and snow, and grey skies.

A: It's unusually cold for the time of year here, too. Here we are, room Alexandre Dumas. Can I take your coat?

B: Thanks.

A: Would you like something to drink? Water? Coffee?

B: Just a sip of water would be nice, thanks.

A: Still or sparkling?

B: Sparkling, please. And would you have a few ice cubes?

A: Sure. I'll be back in a minute.

Nice to meet you. Enchanté !

to stretch one's legs se dégourdir les jambes

a restroom des toilettes

Ready to roll. Allons-y !

the stairs les escaliers

to do *(did, done)* a little sightseeing faire un peu de tourisme

to expect imaginer

the harbour le port

to be *(was, been)* worth sth valoir qqch

awful affreux

slush la neige fondue

the time of year la saison

a coat un manteau

a sip of sth une petite gorgée de qqch

still / sparkling water l'eau plate / gazeuse

ice cubes des glaçons

Useful phrases

- How was your journey here today?
- Did you travel by car? Was the traffic good today?
- Is this your first visit to the area / the company?
- Did you find us easily enough?
- How long will you be staying in France?
- I'm afraid you're a little unlucky with the weather. How is the weather in Florida at the moment?
- Well, it looks like we'll have some nice weather during your stay.

enough assez
to be *(was, been)* unlucky ne pas avoir de chance
it looks like … on dirait que…
a stay une visite

If you're the visitor, naturally your responses should be upbeat and cheerful and you should have some questions and phrases of your own up your sleeve.

- The journey was very good, thanks. Ms Smith's directions were very clear.
- Yes, it's my first time here. I'm hoping to see a little of the local area during my stay.
- Has the company been situated here long?
- The company seems to be very conveniently located. Does it take long to travel into the city from here?
- It's much warmer here than where I've travelled from. Is this weather usual for the time of year?
- At home, it's lovely and warm. It's spring-like!

- It's pouring / coming down in torrents / buckets.
- It's absolutely freezing / boiling.

to be *(was, were)* upbeat être positif, optimiste

to be *(was, were)* cheerful être de bonne humeur

of your own à vous, qui vous appartient

to have *(had, had)* sth up one's sleeve avoir qqch en réserve

warm chaud

spring-like printanier

to pour / to come *(came, come)* down in torrents / buckets pleuvoir à verse, tomber des cordes

It's freezing / boiling! On meurt de froid / chaud !

Introducing oneself and others
Les présentations

When you reach your destination, be sure to thank the person who has shown you the way before they go. The next step will be to introduce yourself to your host and the other meeting attendees. It is usual to shake hands as you do so.

to reach atteindre, parvenir à

to shake *(shook, shaken)* sb's hand serrer la main de qqn

as you do so par la même occasion

'How do you do?' and 'How are you?'
Comment saluer

'How do you do?' is a standard phrase people use when meeting for the first time. It is very polite and more formal than 'Pleased to meet you.' Although this sounds like a question, the required response is: 'How do you do?' In the US, people meeting for the first time sometimes substitute 'How do you do?' for 'How are you?' (response: 'How are you?'). This phrase is also becoming more widely used in UK business culture. The phrase 'Nice to meet you' also exists and is a little less formal than the alternatives above. 'Pleased to meet you' is more appropriate in a business setting. When people who have met on previous occasions ask 'How are you?', the usual response is: 'Fine, thanks, and you?' or, more formally, 'Very well, thank you, and you?'. Americans might also reply 'Good', which may sound a little informal for speakers of UK English.

although bien que

to sound like ressembler à, s'apparenter à

to substitute sth for sth remplacer qqch par qqch

widely largement

a business setting un cadre professionnel

on previous occasions précédemment

Useful phrases

- How do you do? I'm Sylvie Dupuis.
- How do you do, Ms Dupuis? I'm Hilary Smith.
- Hello, I'm Sylvie Dupuis from DEF in France – pleased to meet you.
- Hilary Smith. I'm pleased to meet you, Ms Dupuis.

Nom ou prénom ?

Il est courant d'annoncer à la fois le prénom et le nom de famille quand vous faites les présentations. Cependant, l'usage du prénom est très répandu dans les pays anglophones, même entre personnes de différentes générations ou ne s'étant jamais rencontrées. Si quelqu'un vous appelle par votre prénom, n'hésitez pas à en faire autant. Si vous utilisez le nom de famille, l'usage veut qu'il soit précédé de **Ms** *(« Mademoiselle / Madame » – pour une femme célibataire ou dont vous ignorez si elle est mariée),* **Mrs** *(« Madame » – pour une femme mariée) ou* **Mr** *(« Monsieur » – pour un homme).*

Introducing others
Faire les présentations

There are several ways to introduce other people to one another, depending on the formality of the situation. It is useful to follow the introduction with a line about the person you are introducing. The more formal types of introduction are at the top of the following list and the least formal towards the end.

several nombreux
with a line about ... avec un mot sur...
at the top of ... au début de...
towards the end vers la fin

Useful phrases

- Mr Stevenson, may I introduce Pierre Pirlot? Mr Pirlot is Marketing Director at DEF in Bordeaux.
- Mr Stevenson, I'd like to introduce Pierre Pirlot. Mr Pirlot has come from France to join us for today's meeting.
- Patrick, I'd like you to meet Pierre Pirlot. Pierre is Marketing Director at DEF.
- Patrick, have you met Pierre Pirlot from DEF?
- Patrick, this is Pierre Pirlot, Marketing Director at DEF in France.
- Patrick Stevenson – Pierre Pirlot.
- Patrick – Pierre. Pierre – Patrick.

Small talk

Parler de choses et d'autres

As is well known, it is customary for business partners in English-speaking countries to make some small talk before getting down to the business at hand. With someone you have just met for the first time, the aim of small talk is to break the ice and to find out a little about him or her from a business perspective. Generally speaking, the better you know a person, the more topics you can add to the list of small talk subjects. For people who know each other well, the weather tends to be further down the list of small talk topics.

to get ***(got, got*** *Brit.* ***/ gotten*** *Am.)* **down to** passer à

at hand en question

the aim le but

to find ***(found, found)*** **out about** se renseigner sur

to be ***(was, been)*** **further down the list** être en bas du classement

Examples

Example 1: small talk with someone you know well

Parler de choses et d'autres avec une personne que vous connaissez bien

A: Pierre, good to see you again!

B: Same here, Jack! How has life been treating you since we last met? And how is Susanne?

A: Thanks, Susanne is fine. We're going to have twins in July.

B: Congratulations, that's great news.

Example 2: small talk with someone new

Parler de choses et d'autres avec une personne que vous ne connaissez pas encore

```
A: So you also arrived from London, I heard?
B: Yes, that's right. I flew in from Stansted this
morning. Awful traffic on the M11, just one big
traffic jam after the other.
A: I know what you're talking about. I live in
Cambridge and have to take the M11 every morning to
go to work.
B: Poor you! Where exactly are you based?
A: At the Harlow office. Been there for about
18 months now.
B: Do you happen to know Peter Brooks? From accounts.
A: Peter, sure! We used to have adjacent offices.
How do you know Peter?
```

to fly *(flew, flown)* in from ... arriver de... *(par avion)*

a traffic jam un embouteillage

Do you happen to know ...? Est-ce que par hasard vous connaîtriez... ?

accounts le service comptabilité

used to *verbe auxiliaire exprimant une habitude ou qqch faisant référence au passé*

Useful phrases

- Have you travelled far for today's meeting?
- Whereabouts are you / is your company based?
- So, how long have you been with the company? / Have you been at the company long?

- What is your role at the company?

When talking to someone you have met on previous occasions and with whose job and company you are already familiar, you might start by asking the person about how they are. Then look for common ground with regard to other business or work-related topics and industry developments.

- Hi, John. Good to see you. How are you?
- Hello, Mark. How are you settling in in your new role?
- I heard about your promotion to Sales Director. Congratulations!
- Did you attend the technology conference last week? What did you think of ... ?
- I saw your presentation at the annual convention last month – it was really interesting.
- Have you heard that CBC may be merging with Smith Technologies? How would that impact your business?
- Have you been affected by the recent increases in fuel costs at all?

whereabouts où

How long have you been with the company? Depuis combien de temps êtes-vous dans la société ?

already déjà

common ground / shared interest des points communs

to settle in s'installer, prendre ses marques

to merge fusionner

an increase une augmentation

fuel costs le prix du carburant

La poignée de main

La poignée de main est d'usage lors des premières rencontres, mais pas obligatoire à chaque réunion. Tandis que les participants à d'importantes réunions vont probablement se serrer la main en arrivant, dans les situations informelles, les partenaires

> *qui se sont rencontrés à de précédentes occasions et qui se sentent à l'aise dans l'entreprise de l'autre ne se serreront pas forcément la main à chaque fois.*

How's business – and life?
Comment vont les affaires… et la vie ?

A common phrase English-speakers use with people they have met before and with whom they are on informal terms is simply, 'How's business?' This signals your interest in your conversation partner and their company without pushing for any specific information. This phrase leaves it open for your conversation partner to go into as much detail as they wish in their response. Business partners who know each other well may also graduate to small talk topics regarding their private lives.

Useful phrases

- How's the family? Please give / pass on my regards to [name of partner].
- So, how's life treating you?
- Have you been busy of late?
- So, how was your break in Spain?
- Have you managed to get away for a holiday yet?
- Last time we met you were off to the Bahamas. Did you have a good break?

to push for forcer à

to give ***(gave, given)*** **/ pass on one's regards to s.o.** transmettre son bon souvenir à qqn

of late ces derniers temps

to manage to réussir à

to get ***(got, got*** *Brit.* ***/ gotten*** *Am.)* **away for a holiday** partir en vacances

to be ***(was, been)*** **off to** être parti à

Checklist: levels and topics of small talk

Check-list : les différents niveaux et sujets de conversation courants

Situation	*Example small talk topics*
Escorting someone to a meeting	Journey; travel plans while staying in the area; weather
Post-introductions; meeting someone for the first time	Journey; person's role at their company / their work; information about their company / industry; travel plans while staying in the area; weather
Someone you have met before; waiting for the meeting to start	How are you? How's business?; journey; trade fairs / conferences etc; industry developments; events of shared interest: work or business-related; weather
Someone you know well	As level above, and also: family; holidays; news, sports, music events etc.

a trade fair une foire commerciale

Effortless small talk

Briser la glace facilement

To make your small talk more fluent, you should bear some tactics in mind. They will make it easier for your partner to carry on with the small talk, and you will be perceived as a person who takes an interest in others and is open and friendly.

fluent fluide
to carry on continuer
to be *(was, been)* perceived as être perçu comme

Checklist: tactics for effortless small talk

Check-list : comment briser la glace facilement

Tactic	*Example*
Give answers in full sentences.	Where in France are you from? I'm from Perpignan, that's in the south, close to the Spanish border.
Listen for indirect signals.	We had quite a storm on the lake yesterday and almost capsized. So you must be a good sailor?
Give some information about yourself.	I really need to leave the meeting on time. I've to pick up my child at five.

a border une frontière
quite a storm une grosse tempête
to capsize chavirer
a sailor un marin
to pick up s.o. aller chercher qqn

Setting up the meeting room

Préparer la salle de réunion

Even if you reserved the necessary technical items, things don't always run smoothly on the day of the meeting itself. You may need help setting up the equipment – especially if you are using conference call equipment. Ask a technician to check if it is set up properly before the meeting starts.

even if même si

to run *(ran, run)* smoothly bien fonctionner

a conference call une téléconférence

properly correctement

Useful phrases

Asking for help

Demander de l'aide

- I'm afraid this extension lead isn't quite long enough. Could I trouble you for a longer one?
- I'm having a little trouble with the projector. Please could you give me a hand to set it up?
- Is there anywhere I could plug my mobile phone in to charge during the meeting?
- Do you mind if I plug my laptop into this power socket?

Offering help

Proposer de l'aide

- Are you okay with that? Do you need any help at all?
- Can I give you a hand with setting that up?
- Do you need an extension lead for your laptop?
- Just a moment – I'll ask someone from technical support to come and give you a hand with that.

to trouble s.o. déranger qqn

to give *(gave, given)* s.o. a hand to aider qqn à

to plug in brancher

Are you okay with that? Vous vous en sortez ?

Conducting a meeting

Animer une réunion

En plus de jouer un rôle-clé dans la préparation de l'ordre du jour, le président structure la réunion elle-même. Il ou elle cadre la discussion des points à l'ordre du jour en exécutant les formalités d'usage, au début, pendant et à la fin de la réunion.

Dans ce chapitre, vous trouverez plus d'informations sur la façon de :

- Ouvrir la réunion (page 60).
- Mener le débat (page 64).
- Parvenir à une décision (page 70).
- Clore la réunion (page 72).

Opening the meeting

Ouvrir la réunion

The main task of the chair is to make sure the meeting runs smoothly. He or she opens and closes the meeting, manages time, facilitates conversation, assigns tasks and summarises what was achieved during the meeting.

to assign a task to sb confier une tâche à qqn

to summarise résumer

Example: the start of the meeting

Le début de la réunion

```
Chair: Good afternoon, everyone. Before we start,
Sarah Delcourt has asked me to pass on her
apologies: unfortunately she can't make it today
as she's attending the sales conference in Athens.
I would also like to introduce David Bonnet from
ABC Europe who has flown in from Brussels to join
us today. David, could I ask you to tell us briefly
about your role in the project?

DB: Yes, thank you, Brian. I'm heading up the
project team in Brussels. We're a team of six
and we're dealing with the logistics side of the
product launch in Europe.

Chair: Great, thank you, David. For David's
benefit, could we all introduce ourselves, going
anti-clockwise around the table?

[Round of introductions]

Chair: As you all know from the agenda, today's
objective is to agree on the packaging for the new
```

product. Now, we do need to make sure we finish on time this afternoon so that David can make his evening flight back to Brussels. We've allowed 15 minutes for each item on the agenda and a further 20 minutes for questions at the end. So, shall we get straight on with item one?

Useful phrases

- Good morning, ladies and gentlemen. Thank you all for joining us today. Shall we make a start? [Formal]
- Good morning, everyone. Thanks for coming. Shall we get down to business / get the ball rolling? [Informal]

to pass on transmettre
to head up diriger
to deal *(dealt, dealt)* with s'occuper de
a launch un lancement
for s.o.'s benefit dans l'intérêt de qqn
(anti-)clockwise dans le sens (inverse) des aiguilles d'une montre
a further 20 minutes 20 minutes supplémentaires
to get *(got, got* Brit. */ gotten* Am.*)* straight on enchaîner
to make *(made, made)* a start commencer
to get *(got, got* Brit. */ gotten* Am.*)* the ball rolling passer aux choses sérieuses

Introductions and apologies
Les présentations et les absents

At external meetings where the participants do not yet know each other, the chair is likely to start by making formal introductions or asking the participants to introduce themselves.

to be *(was, been)* likely to être susceptible de

Useful phrases

- Perhaps we could start by introducing ourselves, moving clockwise around the table?
- For those of you who haven't yet had the chance to meet, I would like to start by introducing …
- Our presenter today is Solène Cochard. Solène is going to talk to us about ...
- On my left is ...
- Also joining us is ...
- I have received apologies from Olivier Poyer, who is unable to join us today, and Marc Chapal, who will be arriving a little late.
- Has anyone seen Valérie? She's supposed to come, too.

How to say 'I'm sorry'

S'excuser de façon appropriée

Whether to use 'apology' or 'excuse' depends on the situation. In a meeting, you use 'apologies from Paul', meaning that Paul was unable to attend. An 'excuse' can also be used in the sense of the French *prétexte*. In formal English you would say, 'I apologise for being late', in informal English 'I'm sorry I'm late'. In both cases, you would add the reason for being late, e.g. 'My plane was delayed'.

You use 'excuse me' to catch someone's attention, e.g. 'Excuse me, could you pass me the coffee, please?' 'I beg your pardon?' or 'Pardon?' are formal ways of stating that you haven't understood what someone was saying. In informal situations you simply say 'Sorry?'.

delayed retardé
to catch one's attention attirer l'attention de qqn

Introducing the agenda and the objectives of the meeting

Présenter l'ordre du jour et les objectifs de la réunion

Useful phrases

- As you know, we're here today to discuss ...
- The objective / purpose of today's meeting is to reach agreement on ...
- Does everyone have / does anyone need a copy of the agenda?
- We have approximately 15 minutes for each point on the agenda.
- So, moving onto the first item / point on the agenda, ...

Initiating the discussion

Entamer le débat

Useful phrases

- The first agenda item – renewal of company insurance – was put forward by Céline Boucher. Céline, would you like to start us off?
- Simon, you put forward item three on the agenda. Perhaps you could fill us in on this point?
- Justine, could you bring us up to date on item four?
- Brian, would you outline item five for us?
- Pierre, could you fill us in on the background?

as you know comme vous le savez

a renewal un renouvellement, une reconduction

to put *(put, put)* forward émettre, suggérer

to fill s.o. in on sth remplacer qqn pour qqch

to bring *(brought, brought)* s.o. up to date on sth mettre qqn au courant de qqch

to outline exposer brièvement

Guiding the discussion

Mener le débat

It is the chair's responsibility to make sure all the participants have their say – by guiding the discussion, encouraging everyone to speak up and, if necessary, curtailing the flow of speech of individuals who are too vociferous.

Useful phrases

- Thank you, Brian. Pierre, do you have any thoughts on this?
- So, Pierre agrees with Brian regarding this item. Barbara, could I bring you in at this point?
- I'd also like to hear Julie's opinion at this point.
- Could you elaborate on that for us, please?
- Does anyone else have anything to add to this?

to have *(had, had)* one's say dire ce que l'on a à dire

to speak *(spoke, spoken)* up intervenir

to curtail restreindre

to be *(was, been)* vociferous être véhément

to have *(had, had)* thoughts on sth avoir une opinion sur qqch

to bring *(brought, brought)* s.o. in donner la parole à qqn

to elaborate on sth développer qqch

Dealing with dominant participants and interruptions

Répartir le temps de parole entre les principaux participants et autres intervenants

Useful phrases

- Thank you, Laurent. Could I just stop you there for a moment, because I'd like to bring Thierry in here.
- Laurent, could I ask you to let Thierry finish his point and then we can hear your view?
- I'm sorry, Laurent – I'd just like to finish hearing what Thierry has to say on this point and then we'll come back to you.
- I'm sorry, Alexandra, we don't have time to talk about that now, I'm afraid.

to finish one's point finir de s'exprimer

to hear *(heard, heard)* s.o.'s view écouter l'avis de qqn

Les astuces du président

Vous remarquerez que le président exprime ses requêtes sous forme de suggestions ou de questions. Il s'adresse aux participants par leur nom pour être certain de capter leur attention et gère les interruptions avec tact par un **I'm sorry** *(« Je suis désolé »), en assurant la personne concernée qu'elle pourra intervenir juste après.*

Encouraging quiet participants to contribute

Encourager les participants peu loquaces à s'exprimer

Example: facilitating a balanced discussion

Faciliter les échanges équilibrés

Chair: Item one is the font used on the outer packaging. Marc, could you outline the design department's view on this?

Marc: Sure. We've come to the conclusion that Option A is the best choice as it's the most legible against the blue background and consistent ...

David: Can I come in here? I think ...

Chair: Sorry, David, could we just let Marc finish his point and then we'll hear your view.

Marc: ... and it's consistent with the overall branding.

Chair: Thank you, Marc. Did you want to comment on that, David?

David: Yes – in Logistics we strongly prefer Option B. It's far more eye-catching.

Chair: So we have Option A for Design and Option B for Logistics. Sophie, could you please tell us Manufacturing's perspective?

a font une police (de caractères)
legible lisible
consistent cohérent
the overall branding l'image de la marque
eye-catching accrocheur

Useful phrases

- I'd like to ask Patricia to tell us about the new development at this point, if I may.
- Mr Blanchet, what is your opinion here?
- Julien, it would be useful to hear your perspective on this.
- Sandra, how would this affect the HR [Human Resources] department?
- Julie raised the point that our existing contract is about to expire. What's your take on this, Émilie?
- Tiphaine, you've been working with this client for some time now. What do you say to the point Hélène raised?

if I may si je puis me permettre
to raise a point soulever un point
a take un point de vue, une position
for some time depuis assez longtemps
What do you say to ...? Que pensez-vous de... ?

Reminding participants to be brief
Rappeler aux participants d'être concis

Useful phrases

- Before we move on to the next item, could you quickly give us your opinion on this, Marie?
- I'm afraid we have to move on to the next item. Could you bring your point to a close, please?
- I'm afraid I have to stop you there. Time is ticking away.
- Could I ask you to keep your comment brief, please?
- Can I remind you that we only have 15 minutes for each item?

to move on to passer à

Time is ticking away. Le temps passe vite.

Keeping to the agenda

S'en tenir à l'ordre du jour

Example: directing the discussion

Orienter le débat

David: ... and therefore we would be strongly in favour of B, because, as I've already said, we ...

Chair: Could I stop you there for a moment, David? I'm afraid time's running short. Marc, what do you think about item two?

Marc: Design would like to rethink the shape of the packaging. We'd like to make it a little taller, because ...

David: I totally agree. Some years ago we opted for square packaging for another product and it was a total flop. In fact, this particular product was ...

Chair: That's a valid point, David, but I'd like to bring the discussion back to this year's launch if possible ...

Time is running short. Le temps passe vite.

the shape la forme

square carré

valid valable

Useful phrases

- I think we risk moving away from the agenda here. Could we bring the discussion back to ...?
- We have a lot to cover this morning – I'm afraid we don't have time to go into that. Can we focus on ...?
- I'm afraid we're getting sidetracked. Let's return to …
- That's an important point, but I think that's a discussion for another day. I'd like to go on with the sales figures.
- That's a valid point. May we come back to that later?

to move away from sth s'éloigner de qqch
to focus on se concentrer sur
to get *(got, got* *Brit.* / ***gotten* *Am.)* sidetracked** s'égarer *(fig.)*

Summarising and concluding an item
Résumer et conclure un point

Useful phrases

- So, we've established that the July deadline is too ambitious. What is a more realistic target?
- So, just in order to summarise / sum up / recap what we've said, ...
- So, to bring this point to a close, we can say that ...
- So, am I right in concluding that we'll ... ?
- I think we've agreed / we're all in agreement that ...

Moving on to the next agenda item
Passer au point suivant

Useful phrases

- The next point / item two on today's agenda is ...
- I'd like to move on to item three now.
- Now, turning to item four, ...
- Anyway, about the new location …

to turn to passer à

a new location un nouvel emplacement

Bringing about a decision
Parvenir à une décision

The purpose of most meetings is not only to exchange information, but also to reach decisions. If a decision does not come about naturally, the chair might have to 'push' the participants to make up their minds. Sometimes it may also be necessary to postpone taking a decision.

to come *(came, come)* about arriver, se produire

to make *(made, made)* up one's mind se décider

How to reach consensus
Comment parvenir à un accord

Attendees need sufficient time to express their opinions. Nobody likes to be rushed into a decision. Minority views should receive ample attention so that their owners feel they were heard. A short break often helps to bring about a decision.

Summarising the general mood at the end of each item on the agenda contributes to a clear outcome. Every attendee is more aware of what the general views are. The chair can also help the participants reach a decision by phrasing questions carefully. If the chair has the feeling that there are more outspoken supporters in favour of an issue, they should ask: 'Does anyone object?' rather than 'Does everyone approve?'

to be *(was, been)* rushed into a decision être bousculé pour prendre une décision

often souvent

the general mood l'état d'esprit général

the outcome le résultat

to be *(was, been)* aware of être conscient de

carefully prudemment

outspoken franc, direct

to object élever une objection

Example: summarising and bringing about a conclusion

Résumer et parvenir à une conclusion

Chair: So, to sum up item five, we've agreed that we're going to opt for silver packaging. The next item on the agenda is 'Cardboard or plastic packaging'. We've already heard everyone's views on this topic, so could we move straight to a show of hands for cardboard? That's six. Thank you. For the minutes, that's a majority decision in favour of cardboard.

Useful phrases

- Could we make a yes or no decision on this item? Could all those in favour please raise their hands?
- Could we have a show of hands for going ahead with the measure, please?
- Am I right in saying that we've decided in favour of / against this move?
- So we have decided to commission Union Brothers with the catering for the event.
- Is it okay with everybody to bring the launch forward by two weeks?
- It would certainly be wrong to rush into a decision. Could we leave this until another time?

silver argent *(matière, couleur)*
cardboard du carton
a show of hands un vote à main levée
to raise one's hand lever la main
to go *(went, gone)* ahead with sth mettre qqch à exécution
against contre
to commission s.o. with sth charger qqn de qqch
the catering la restauration

Closing the meeting
Clore la réunion

Initiating further action
Amorcer une action future

Before the meeting closes, all the 'to dos' should be allocated. In the closing remarks, the chairperson or participants may also wish to discuss the date and time for the next meeting, when the minutes will be available or the date by which a decision should be made.

Example: allocating follow-up tasks
Assigner des tâches de suivi

Chair: Marc has kindly offered to follow this up with the shipping department. Can you do this before next week's meeting, Marc?

Marc: Yes, no problem.

Chair: Great. Can somebody volunteer to contact the supplier before next week? David? Thank you. We're almost out of time, but does anyone have any last questions before we finish? No? Well, so we can finish the meeting. Thank you all for coming and for your input. I wish David a safe flight back to Brussels.

the 'to dos' les choses à faire
the shipping department le service des expéditions
a supplier un fournisseur

to be *(was, been)* out of time ne plus avoir de temps
Thank you for your input. Merci pour votre participation.

Useful phrases

- We need somebody to contact the supplier. Ian, could you do this for us?
- Ophélie has offered to file the application. How long do you think this process will take, Ophélie?
- Could you follow this up for us, please?

- Thanks for volunteering to do this, Marine. Do you think this will be possible in time for next week's meeting?
- Jérôme, when will you be able to email out today's minutes to everyone?
- Manon, do you think you could get back to us on that tomorrow by email?
- We'll meet again on the first of next month.
- I'll send out a group email with the minutes tomorrow.
- Can we fix the date for the next meeting, please?
- So, the next meeting will be on next Tuesday.
- What about the following Wednesday? How is that for everyone?

to file an application déposer une demande

to be *(was, been)* able to pouvoir

How is that for everyone? Cela convient-il à tout le monde ?

Bringing the meeting to a close

Annoncer la fin de la réunion

There are different reasons why a meeting comes to an end. Time may have run out or all of the items on the agenda may have been checked off. Some meetings will end earlier than expected and others will run late. Before the chair closes the meeting, he or she will let the participants know the meeting is drawing to a close.

to be *(was, been)* checked off être coché

to run *(run, run)* late être en retard

to draw *(drew, drawn)* to a close toucher à sa fin

Useful phrases

Formal meetings

- I am officially ending today's meeting. You will receive the minutes within two days.
- I declare the meeting closed.
- The meeting is adjourned until tomorrow, 8.00 a.m.

Informal meetings

- It looks like we've run out of time.
- Before we bring the meeting to a close, does anyone have any other business to discuss?
- Well, we're almost out of time for today. Are there any last questions before we finish?
- Is there any other business?
- I think we've covered everything on the agenda.
- As you can all see from the agenda, that was the last item. If no one has anything else to add, then I think we'll wrap this up.
- That brings us to the end of the meeting.
- Let's call it a day, then.
- The meeting is closed.

to wrap up conclure
Let's call it a day. C'est tout pour aujourd'hui.

Thanking the attendees

Remercier les participants

Thanking the participants is usually one of the last remarks. However, even after closing the meeting the chairperson might realise they have forgotten something. There is almost always one last thing to say.

Useful phrases

- I'd like to thank you all for coming and I wish you a safe journey back.
- Thank you all for your participation.
- I'd especially like to thank Karl for coming over from Glasgow.
- Oh, before you leave, please make sure you have signed the attendance sheet.
- Could I have your attention again, please? I didn't mention that ...
- If you could all return your chairs to the room next door that would be much appreciated.

the attendance sheet la feuille d'émargement

to return sth to rapporter qqch à / dans

The meeting itself

La réunion en elle-même

Divers rôles et objectifs font leur apparition lors d'une réunion. Le président est chargé de faire en sorte qu'elle soit agréable et intéressante. Cependant, participer demande une véritable maîtrise des différents registres de langue. La plus grande difficulté se fait surtout sentir lorsqu'on se lance sur le terrain de la politesse et de la diplomatie.

Dans ce chapitre, vous trouverez des informations sur comment :

- Distribuer et accepter les rôles (page 78).
- Écouter attentivement et poser des questions (page 80).
- Exprimer son accord et son désaccord (page 87).
- Faire des suggestions et donner son opinion (page 98).
- Demander s'il reste des incompréhensions et les lever (page 101).
- Faire preuve de diplomatie et de politesse (page 106).
- Pallier un problème de compréhension (page 113).
- Voter (page 114).

Roles at a meeting
Le rôle de chaque participant lors d'une réunion

Whether your meeting is formal or informal, it will run more smoothly if one of the participants assumes the role of chair (See *Conducting a meeting*, p. 59).

Other important players at the meeting are the minute-taker and the participants. The minute-taker writes the minutes, i.e. he or she records the meeting and keeps track of what has been said. One could also say that the minute-taker is the administrator for the meeting.

The participants can take various roles, such as the role of the presenter, who provides information, or the role of a task owner, meaning that an individual is in charge of a certain topic. Participants are also thinking resources – they contribute ideas, help to solve problems and shed light on issues from different perspectives.

a player un acteur
the minute-taker le secrétaire de séance
i.e. ***(id est)*** c-à-d *(c'est-à-dire)*
to record enregistrer
to keep ***(kept, kept)*** **track of** suivre
such as tel / telle que, comme
a task owner une personne ayant la charge d'un sujet
to shed ***(shed, shed)*** **light on sth** éclaircir qqch

Assigning and accepting roles
Confier ou accepter un rôle

For formal meetings, the above roles will usually be allocated before the meeting itself. At more informal meetings, one of the chair's first tasks during the meeting may be to assign these roles to other participants.

If this role has not been assigned yet – which usually happens in the run-up to the meeting, as the minute-taker should prepare in advance (writing equipment, preliminary information etc.) – perhaps the easiest way is to ask for volunteers.

Example: asking for a minute-taker

Recruter un secrétaire de séance

Chair: Do I have any volunteers for minute-taker today? Don't all jump at once! No volunteers? Okay. Pierre, could I ask you to take the minutes today?

Pierre: I'm afraid I'm pretty tied up this week - I don't think I'd be able to turn them around in time for the next meeting.

Chair: No problem. How about Sarah?

Sarah: I'm sorry, but I'm on a training course in the Manchester office all next week.

Chair: I see. Jacques, do you have time to do the minutes?

Jacques: Yes, certainly.

the run-up to la dernière ligne droite avant

Don't all jump at once! Ne répondez pas tous à la fois !

to turn sth around renvoyer qqch

a training course un stage de formation

In the above example, two participants use the following polite formulations to decline the chair's request: 'I'm afraid', 'I'm sorry, but ...' Notice how the chair continues to ask around the group until this important role has been assigned.

Useful phrases

- Do I have any volunteers for taking the minutes today?
- Who would like to be our minute-taker this morning?
- Guillaume, could I ask you to be minute-taker today?
- Jeanne, would you be so kind as to take the minutes for us?

until jusqu'à
to be *(was, been)* so kind as avoir la gentillesse de

Active participation and asking for more information

Participation active et demande d'informations supplémentaires

While it is the chair's job to manage the meeting, meeting participants also have an active role to play to aid communication and make the meeting as effective as possible. Asking questions is an effective method of obtaining more in-depth information, while active listening shows the person you are talking to that you are paying attention and have understood what they are saying.

effective efficace
in-depth approfondi

Interrupting politely

Interrompre poliment

Sometimes you may need to interrupt a speaker in order to ask your question before they move on to another point. Perhaps the speaker has finished his point and there is a natural pause in which you can ask your question.

> ***Excusez-moi !***
> *Employer l'expression* **Sorry!** *(« Excusez-moi ! ») est le moyen le plus facile et le plus rapide d'attirer l'attention poliment et d'interrompre l'orateur. Ces « mots magiques » doivent néanmoins être suivis par ce que vous souhaitez réellement savoir. Si vous voulez seulement vérifier que vous avez bien compris ce qui a été dit, utilisez des expressions comme :* **Sorry – how much did you say?** *(« Excusez-moi, combien avez-vous dit ? ») ou* **Sorry, when did you say?** *(« Excusez-moi, pourriez-vous répéter la date ? »).*

Useful phrases

Formal meetings

- Sorry, I'd just like to ask a question, if I may?
- Sorry, could I interrupt you for a moment? I'd like to ask a question.
- Excuse me, Pierre, I wonder if I could interrupt you for a second?
- Sorry, could I come in here with a question?

Informal meetings

- Sorry to interrupt, but I have a question.

If, on the other hand, you are the speaker, you can prevent an interruption by either just ignoring the person or by saying one of the following phrases:

- Sorry, Jean, can you hear me out, please?
- Just let me finish, please.
- No, Marie, please hear me out.

Could I come in here? Puis-je intervenir ?
on the other hand ... d'autre part...
to prevent éviter
either ... or ... soit... soit...
to hear *(heard, heard)* s.o. out écouter qqn jusqu'au bout

Asking for more information
Demander des informations supplémentaires

Once you have politely gained the speaker's attention, move straight on to your question. Asking for a person's opinion when you ask them a question – for example, 'What do you think will happen?' rather than 'What will happen?' – helps 'soften' the question and makes it less direct. Notice, too, how the questioner below uses 'would' and 'could' instead of the more direct 'will' and 'can'.

to gain one's attention gagner l'attention de qqn
to move straight on to passer rapidement à
to soften atténuer, adoucir

Example: asking for and receiving further information
Demander et obtenir davantage d'informations

A: Moving into the spring, we need to reassess the product range. Then, in the summer, we'll turn our attention to ...

```
B: Sorry, could I interrupt you there for a second?

A: Sure.

B: I have a question: you mentioned reassessing
the product range in the spring. Could I ask you to
expand on that?

A: No problem. Sales of C123 and C124 dropped
dramatically last year, so we want to look at the
reasons for this and perhaps make some adjustments
to the range.

B: Do you mean introducing new products?

A: Actually, it's more likely that some products
will be discontinued.

B: I see. What timescale do you have in mind for
this process?

A: Well, we're planning to start the assessment
in the first week of March and we anticipate that
we'll be finished by mid-April.

B: Right. That's good to know - thank you.
```

the spring le printemps
to reassess réexaminer
the product range la gamme de produits
the summer l'été
to turn one's attention to porter son attention sur
to expand on sth développer, s'étendre sur qqch
to drop chuter
to discontinue supprimer, cesser
a timescale une durée, un délai, un calendrier

Useful phrases

- You mentioned that [repeat the key point]. Could you expand on that for us?
- Could you elaborate / go into more detail on that for us?

- Could you explain that in a little more detail?
- I'm afraid I don't quite follow you there. Could you be a little more precise / specific?
- How do you think that will affect ...?
- What do you think would be the outcome of that?
- What do you consider to be the highest priority here?
- How do you envisage implementing ...?
- What is the timescale likely to be for that / what is the anticipated timescale for this?
- Do you foresee any problems / issues / difficulties there?
- What do you think would be the possible repercussions of that?

to implement mettre en application

to foresee *(foresaw, foreseen)* prévoir

Active listening
Écouter activement

If you don't want to interrupt the speaker's flow, active listening can simply take the form of single words or 'polite noises', such as 'okay', 'aha', 'oh', 'mmm'. Body language, such as nodding and smiling from time to time, should of course accompany all your polite utterings to show that you are listening. Use the handy phrases on next page if you want to signal to the person speaking that you understand.

polite noises des onomatopées courtoises

to nod hocher la tête

utterings des expressions verbales

handy utile

Useful phrases

- I see.
- I understand.
- Right.
- That's interesting.
- Oh, really?
- That makes sense.
- Okay, thank you for explaining that.

Responding to questions
Répondre aux questions

If you need a couple of seconds to think before answering a question, one trick is to repeat the asker's question and clarify what they want to know while you gather your thoughts. When a speaker needs more time to think, they may also try to ask a question back. Maybe they don't have a good answer up their sleeve right away. In this case, they can simply acknowledge the question and play for time before giving a real answer. English-speakers frequently also introduce their answers by starting with, 'Well ...'.

a trick une astuce

to have *(had, had)* a good answer up one's sleeve avoir une bonne réponse sous le coude

to acknowledge prendre note

to play for time essayer de gagner du temps

Example: buying time to think and respond
Gagner du temps pour réfléchir avant de répondre

```
A: So, how do you see this measure taking shape?
B: How do we see the measure taking shape? Well,
first of all, we plan to ...
```

Useful phrases

- I'm not quite sure what you mean by that. Could you explain?
- It all depends on what you mean by the 'extra costs' you mentioned.
- That's a very good question.
- I'm glad you asked that.
- It's hard to say.

Or, perhaps you've been caught on the back foot by an awkward question you weren't quite expecting and need to politely decline to answer.

- I'm afraid I'm not in a position to / able to comment on that / answer that question just now.
- Well, it's rather difficult to say at present.
- I don't have enough information at my disposal to consider all the implications at the moment.
- Maybe we could leave the legal issues aside for a moment, the real challenge for ACME is on the European level.

to be *(was, been)* caught on the back foot être pris de court
awkward difficile

to decline to answer refuser de répondre
legal issues les questions légales
aside à part, de côté

Expressing agreement and disagreement

Exprimer son accord ou son désaccord

In English-speaking cultures, politeness and tact are key elements when expressing approval and disapproval of other people's suggestions and ideas. When expressing disagreement – the more sensitive of the two areas – many English-speakers, and particularly the British, tend towards understatement and often use diplomacy so as not to sound impolite.

Agreeing with an opinion

Être d'accord avec une idée

Example: expressing agreement

Exprimer son accord

A: So, I really think we should wait until next year to launch the campaign.

B: I couldn't agree more. I can't see how launching a new model this late in the season will benefit the range.

C: You're quite right – we could put the remainder of this year's budget to far better use.

A: Well, I'm glad we're all agreed on that.

to tend towards avoir tendance à

an understatement une exagération, un euphémisme

the remainder le reste

a far better use un bien meilleur usage

> ***Différences culturelles entre les États-Unis et la Grande-Bretagne***
> *Bien que la politesse soit importante dans les deux cultures, les Américains seraient plus avenants et directs que leurs homologues britanniques lorsqu'il s'agit d'exprimer leur accord, et plus encore leur désaccord.*

Useful phrases

Total agreement

Accord total

- I couldn't agree with you more.
- You're absolutely right (there).
- I totally / completely / fully / absolutely agree (with you on that point).
- I'm in total agreement with that.

Neutral agreement

Accord neutre

- I agree.
- I would agree with that.
- I'm with you on that.
- I think you're right.
- That's a fair point.
- That's true.

Mild agreement

Accord modéré

- I tend to agree.
- Maybe you're right.

- I suppose so.
- Possibly.
- Could be.

That's a fair point. C'est juste.
That's true. C'est vrai.

I tend to agree. Je suis plutôt d'accord.
Could be. Peut-être.

Diplomatic disagreement
Désaccord et diplomatie

In English-speaking cultures, disagreeing without putting forward an alternative solution is generally viewed as unhelpful. Therefore, the emphasis is on what is known as constructive criticism, which essentially involves coupling disagreement with an alternative suggestion and backing it up with good reasons. So, people often handle disagreement by highlighting an element of an idea they find positive before moving on to tactfully express disagreement with another aspect.

to put *(put, put)* forward proposer
to back up appuyer, soutenir

to handle sth faire face à qqch
to highlight mettre l'accent sur

Example: disagreeing diplomatically
Exprimer son désaccord avec diplomatie

A: I hear what you're saying about that but I do have some reservations about the timing.

B: I see. Could you be more specific?

A: Well, we have the international sales conference coming up in September. Surely we should aim to finish the proposal by then so that we can discuss it at the conference.

B: That's a good point, but I think rushing the proposal to finish it before the conference could be counterproductive.

A: I'm just a little concerned that the Spanish sales team will be left out of the discussion completely if the issue isn't addressed at the conference.

B: I take your point, but I think we'll struggle to compile all the data we need by September.

A: Oh, I see. In that case, what about putting together an overview of the proposal in time for the conference and then scheduling a meeting to discuss it in full at a later date?

B: Yes, that would work.

to aim to avoir pour but de
by then d'ici là
to rush sth faire qqch dans l'urgence
to be *(was, been)* concerned that être inquiet de
to take *(took, taken)* one's point comprendre le point de vue de qqn
to struggle se battre, lutter
data des données
an overview une vue d'ensemble
to work fonctionner

Useful phrases

- I like what you said about the book launch, but I feel we might need to rethink some aspects of it.
- I think the concept is good overall, but I'm not entirely convinced about the marketing element.
- I'm concerned that advertising in this way won't achieve our objective, because ... Have you thought about the possibility of ...?
- My only concern with that is that we could run out of time. Have you considered trying ...?

overall dans l'ensemble

concern l'inquiétude

When 'yes' means 'no'
Quand « oui » signifie « non »

The American culture is what is known as a low-context culture. In such cultures, it is considered most effective to formulate statements in an unambiguous and direct way. In high-context cultures, such as in Britain, non-verbal communication, including body language, plays a more important role. High-context culture speakers are often reluctant to say 'no' in a straightforward way, so be sensitive to 'yes, but' statements that really mean 'no':

- Yes, I take your point, but ...
- Yes, I agree with you, but ...
- Yes, I see what you're saying / what you mean, but ...

When you want to answer in the affirmative way, there are many possibilities besides a simple 'yes'. The same applies to 'no' and 'maybe', as you can see from the following table.

Alternatives to the words 'yes', 'maybe' and 'no'	
Yes	sure certainly of course right hmm yeah okay fine I am / I was / I did I think so absolutely

Alternatives to the words 'yes', 'maybe' and 'no'	
Maybe	perhaps could be I don't know it's hard to say I'm not sure
No	not really I don't think so not just now / not at the moment I'm not / I wasn't / I didn't not completely

to be *(was, been)* reluctant to être réticent à

straightforward franc, clair

a statement une déclaration

maybe peut-être

Degrees of disagreement

Les degrés de désaccord

Bear in mind that, out of politeness, particularly British speakers tend towards understatement in their expression of disagreement. Therefore, phrases that express mild disagreement often conceal opinions that are stronger than they sound. If you're the speaker, remember that toning down your statements a touch will still have the required effect.

Example: various grades of disagreement

Les différents niveaux de désaccord

A: Yes, I agree, but that target is fairly unrealistic based on last year's figures.

B: I'm not sure I agree there. As we said, last year's turnover was down due to external factors beyond our control.

```
A: Yes, but that's not to say that the targets
weren't too high in the first place.
B: I beg to differ. We were on track to hit our
targets before the general downturn in the industry.
A: I see what you're saying, but surely our
targets should have allowed some leeway for that
possibility.
C: I totally disagree. Sales have increased year on
year for the past five years ...
```

to conceal dissimuler

to tone down adoucir le ton de, atténuer

fairly clairement

beyond one's control qui ne dépend pas de qqn

I beg to differ. Je ne suis pas d'accord.

to be *(was, been)* on track to do sth chercher à / être sur le point de faire qqch

leeway la liberté de manœuvre

Checklist: disagreement

Check-list : le désaccord

1. Politeness and diplomacy are key.
2. Bear understatement in mind, both when interpreting other people's statements of disagreement and formulating your own. Making your statements milder will still get your point across in the English-speaking world.
3. If possible, highlight any items you agree with before being specific about the aspects you disagree with.
4. Use constructive criticism: always try to put forward alternative solutions to problems.
5. Back up disagreement with good reasons.
6. 'Yes, but' statements are a tactful way to say 'no'.

to get ***(got, got*** *Brit.* ***/ gotten*** *Am.)* **a point across** faire passer une idée

Useful phrases

Mild disagreement

Désaccord modéré

- I'm not sure about that.
- I'm not sure I agree.
- I'm not totally convinced about that.
- I hesitate to agree with you there, because ...

Neutral disagreement

Désaccord neutre

- I'm sorry, but I can't agree on that point.
- I'm afraid I don't agree.
- I tend to disagree.
- I beg to differ.

Strong disagreement

Désaccord total

If a speaker strongly disagrees with a standpoint, 'softeners', such as 'I'm afraid', 'I'm sorry, but' tend to fall away:

- I totally disagree.
- I don't agree at all.
- I'm in complete disagreement with you.
- To the contrary, I think ...

a standpoint un point de vue
to fall *(fell, fallen)* away s'effacer

Expressing criticism
Émettre des critiques

As with disagreement, diplomacy is called for when it comes to expressing criticism in the English-speaking world. English-speakers often tone down criticism by using a positive word in the negative, rather than a negative word:

- not very good: bad
- not up to standard: below standard
- not very encouraging: disappointing.

to call for exiger
not to be *(was, been)* up to standard ne pas avoir le niveau requis
disappointing décevant

Atténuer les critiques
La critique est souvent mieux reçue si elle est exprimée avec diplomatie. En anglais, pour adoucir une déclaration, essayez d'utiliser des expressions comme :
not quite / not really + *un mot positif (ex.* **adequate***) ou*
a little / somewhat + *un mot négatif (ex.* **disappointing***).*

Criticism: can you read between the lines?

What is said	What is meant
This isn't quite what we were expecting. This falls a little below our expectations.	This doesn't meet our expectations at all.
The design isn't quite what we were hoping for. The design is not exactly what we were looking for.	We don't like it at all.
Their performance isn't really up to scratch. Their performance is a little under par.	Their performance is not acceptable.

not to be *(was, been)* up to scratch ne pas être à la hauteur

to be *(was, been)* under par être en dessous de la moyenne

Straight talking

Le franc-parler

Despite your best efforts to put your point across tactfully, sometimes there are situations which call for a more direct approach. In English, unpleasant news is often preceded by short phrases which brace the listener for what is to come.

Example: let's face facts

Regardons les choses en face

A: I accept that sales were a little lower than expected.

B: Let's not beat around the bush: they were very disappointing.

```
A: Frankly, I think that's overstating it a little.
Those kinds of figures are to be expected in the
current business climate.
B: Look, I think we should face facts: the product
is just not performing as we planned. To be honest,
I think it's time we pulled the plug ...
```

Useful phrases

- Let's not beat around the bush ...
- Let's face facts ...
- Let's be honest ...
- Let's get one thing straight ...
- To be honest, I ...
- Frankly, I ...
- I don't want to rock the boat / upset the applecart, but ...
- I don't want to paint too black a picture, but ...

to brace s.o. for préparer qqn à
to beat *(beat, beaten)* around the bush tourner autour du pot
to overstate exagérer
to pull the plug se retirer, abandonner
to rock the boat / to upset the applecart tout saboter / tout gâcher

Making suggestions and having your say

Faire des suggestions et donner son avis

Example: making suggestions

Faire des suggestions

A: I would advise the Board to slash the budget for tobacco advertising. That way, we are on the safe side.

B: Why do you think that?

A: The new EU directive poses an immediate threat to our market share.

B: In my view this prospective danger is still in the stars. What I think is that we should deal with the problems at hand, rather than musing about what might happen in ten years' time!

A: I'm not dodging the issue of teenage smoking, if this is what you mean. On the contrary! We'll have to face the music sooner or later. I assure you that I do care about the issue.

to slash réduire

to pose a threat constituer une menace

to be *(was, been)* in the stars être abstrait

to muse about songer à, réfléchir à

to dodge esquiver

to face the music affronter la tempête

Informal formulations and questions for making suggestions are also suitable for meetings. A more tentative way of making a suggestion includes 'would', 'could' or 'might / may'.

Useful phrases

- Why don't we try …?
- Let's take a novel approach in this matter.
- Shall we …?
- May / might I suggest we stick to our initial plan?
- Wouldn't it be worth trying to give a new supplier a chance?
- Could there be another way forward?

Expressing your opinion

Exprimer son avis

Of course, you can simply state your opinion by plainly saying what you mean. You would usually use an introductory phrase like 'I suggest' or 'I would advise that …'

In a discussion, your tone of voice and intonation would of course also influence the way your opinions come across. Quite naturally, the point you want to make should be pronounced more emphatically than the rest of the sentence. Another way of emphasising and adding stress is to use auxiliaries that you would not need for grammatical reasons.

a tentative way of… une manière modérée de…

a way forward une solution

to come *(came, come)* across transparaître

to add stress accentuer

Useful phrases

Neutral expression of an opinion

Exprimer son opinion de façon neutre

- I suggest that we reconsider our standpoint.
- My proposal is to start negotiations as fast as we can.

Strong expression of an opinion

Exprimer son opinion très clairement

- I strongly recommend investing in commodities.
- It is high time we became active in this field.
- I advise all of you to reconsider your views.
- There's no alternative to buying new machines.
- It's not a rumour, our competitors are launching the new storage system, that's a fact.
- I do think it's important to meet before the 17th!

However, the best phrases won't make an impact unless your entire performance radiates confidence. Here are some tips.

as fast as aussi vite que

commodities des produits, des matières premières

the storage l'entreposage, la mémoire (informatique)

unless à moins que

to radiate confidence respirer la confiance

Checklist: how to have your say

Check-list : comment parvenir à exprimer son point de vue

1. Try to avoid a thin voice, hurrying or stuttering – there's no need to be afraid.
2. There's no need to hesitate if you know your point is valid. If you are not sure yourself, say that you are not sure.
3. Look at the group: make eye contact with everyone in the group, don't avoid it by looking at the ceiling, the flipchart, the walls ...
4. Play with your voice: emphasise important points, breathe deeply to make your voice stronger, make your voice more interesting by modulating your pitch.

5 Express yourself accurately: no generalisations, avoid words like 'never', 'always', 'everyone'.

6 Keep your hands and feet still – no fiddling or fidgeting.

stuttering balbutiant
the ceiling le plafond
the flipchart le tableau (à feuilles)
to breathe deeply respirer profondément
the pitch le ton *(d'une voix)*
accurately avec précision
still immobile
to fiddle tripoter
to fidget ne pas tenir en place

Useful grammar

Don't forget that question tags may also be used to make a statement more palatable to your counterpart and to urge him or her to react. Note that a negative tag asks for agreement, whereas a positive tag shows that you are looking to your counterpart to share your disagreement.

- I think April is a good month for team trainings, don't you?
- Mr Ménard isn't the right person for the job, is he?

palatable acceptable
a counterpart un homologue
to urge sb to pousser qqn à
to share partager

Enquiring and resolving misunderstandings

Demander s'il subsiste des incompréhensions et les lever

Remember, it is always better to resolve a misunderstanding immediately so that it cannot lead to problems later or cause the meeting to drift off in a completely different direction. One way to check the facts is to ask for them again.

to lead (led, led) to mener à

to drift off dériver

Asking for repetition

Demander à ce que l'on répète

Example: sorry?

Excusez-moi ?

A: So, overall, the figures for ... [sound of loud drilling outside]

B: I'm sorry, it's terribly noisy with the window open. I didn't hear your last point. Could you run through it again, please?

A: [speaks very quickly] I was just saying that until we look at the figures we just aren't in a position to know if it actually made a difference to the bottom line and it would be premature to move onto A3 without taking this step. We really should hold fire on this for a while.

B: Okay, so just to clarify, by A3 you're referring to the summer promotion?

A: That's right.

B: I'm not sure I fully understand the point you were making about A3.

A: In a nutshell, we need to gauge the success of the previous promotion before launching the new one.

B: I see - and yes, I totally agree.

drilling le perçage, le forage

to run *(ran, run)* through reprendre, récapituler

to hold *(held, held)* fire on sth suspendre qqch, garder qqch de côté

for a while pendant quelque temps

in a nutshell en un mot

to gauge mesurer, évaluer

A good way to ask your counterpart for repetition or clarification of what they said is to use the following question words:

- *What* did you say?
- *Who* did you say?
- *When* did you say?
- *Why* did you say?
- *How many / much* did you say?

Useful phrases

- I'm sorry, I didn't quite catch that / the last thing you said.
- I'm sorry, it's a little noisy outside. I didn't hear what you just said.
- I'm sorry, could you speak a little louder, please?
- I'm sorry, would you mind repeating that last point, please?
- I'm sorry, could you repeat your first point for me, please?
- Sorry, could you explain that again, please?
- I'm afraid I'm not quite clear what you mean.
- Sorry, I don't quite follow you.
- Sorry, I'm not sure I understood. Would you mind going over that again?

to catch *(caught, caught)* comprendre, saisir

a little louder un peu plus fort

to go *(went, gone)* over sth again revenir sur qqch

Would you mind ...? Pourriez-vous… ?

Summarising for clarification

Résumer pour éclaircir un point

Another good way to check your understanding is to reformulate the speaker's point in your own words.

Useful phrases

- Are you saying that you can't deliver next week?
- Correct me if I'm wrong, but …
- Did I get it right that …?
- Have I understood you right? Do you mean …?
- So, just to check I understand you correctly, do you mean …?
- Just to clarify, do you mean …?
- So, just to make sure we're all singing from the same hymn sheet, you're saying that …
- To quickly summarise, your point is that …
- Just to recap, are you saying that …?

Did I get it right that…? Ai-je bien compris que… ?

to sing *(sang, sung)* from the same hymn sheet être sur la même longueur d'onde

La double question

En anglais, les orateurs utilisent souvent une double question pour vérifier ce qu'une personne a dit ou pour s'assurer de ce qu'ils ont compris. Par exemple :

Warranty? What exactly do you mean by warranty? *(« Une garantie ? Qu'entendez-vous exactement par garantie ? »)*

> **Whereabouts is Kemer? I mean, how far is it to the nearest airport?** *(« Où est Kemer ? Je veux dire, à quelle distance se trouve t-il de l'aéroport le plus proche ? »)*

Recapping and confirming
Récapituler et confirmer

If you're the speaker, you may feel it is important to clarify your point or to check that the other participants have understood.

Useful phrases

- What I meant was ...
- What I mean to say is that ...
- The point I'm making is ...
- Are you with me so far?
- Are you following me?
- Does that make sense?
- Do you understand what I mean?
- I'm afraid that isn't quite what I meant.
- There seems to have been a slight misunderstanding.
- Maybe I didn't make myself clear.
- The point I'm making is that we are wasting a lot of manpower with the old equipment.
- Actually, I am not talking about renting, I am talking about profitability.

Are you with me so far? Est-ce que vous me suivez ?
to waste gaspiller
the manpower la main d'œuvre
renting la location
profitability la rentabilité

Useful grammar

There are specific verbs in the English language that must be followed by a gerund (~ing form). 'To mind' is such a verb. Other verbs and fixed expressions of that kind which are useful for meetings are as follows:

- This would *involve bringing* in an external consultant.
- Shall we *consider expanding* into China?
- I *suggest planning* two years ahead.
- You cannot *avoid taking* risks altogether.
- This *risks spinning* out of control.
- I'm *looking forward to seeing* you.
- I *apologise for being* late.
- We *are thinking about investing* in oil shares.

to spin *(span, spun)* out of control échapper à tout contrôle
oil le pétrole

Diplomacy and politeness
Diplomatie et politesse

It's bad news, I'm afraid …
Annoncer une mauvaise nouvelle

Diplomacy and politeness are not only important elements when it comes to expressing agreement and disagreement in English-speaking meetings. They also come to the fore when English-speakers are about to deliver bad news or present information that they know may not be well received by the listener.

Example: using language to persuade
Utiliser les bons mots pour convaincre

A: Right, we've got some broad agreement on the way forward, but let's now focus on some practical details. Kevin, do you think I could ask your team to do the figures for the presentation?

B: Well, in principle, yes, but this comes as a bit of a surprise.

A: I see. What do you think would be a reasonable deadline?

B: I'm afraid I can't promise anything right now. Shall we say by the day after tomorrow, around noon?

A: That could be cutting it a bit fine - ideally we need the figures tomorrow at 5.00 p.m. at the latest.

B: Let me think. I was wondering if we could speed up the process by outsourcing some of the graphics. Wouldn't it be faster if the charts were done by our colleagues in Brussels? You know, we're all pretty busy with the Wang project, which is already slightly behind schedule.

A: Okay, fair enough. Could you get on to them right away?

to come *(came, come)* to the fore ressortir

broad général

to cut *(cut, cut)* it fine être juste *(au niveau de l'heure)*

to outsource sous-traiter, externaliser

pretty (busy) vraiment (occupé)

to be *(was, been)* slightly behind schedule être légèrement en retard

fair enough très bien

Useful phrases

- I'm afraid it's not good news.
- As (I'm sure) you appreciate, this is a difficult situation.
- I'm sorry to say that ...
- Regrettably, we ...
- Unfortunately ...

Polite questions

La courtoisie avant tout

However, there is more to diplomatic language than just lists of readymade phrases: expressing the matter in a different way, i.e. using little twists with language can help. If you ask a question, e.g., instead of making a statement, your request will sound more sophisticated and less dogmatic; 'would' and 'could' also sound far more polite than 'can' and 'will'.

For example, compare, 'Wouldn't it be a good idea to deliver in two weeks?' with bluntly stating: 'We will deliver in two weeks.' And the longer a sentence is, the more politely it is perceived to be by the listener;

e.g. 'How old is the car?' sounds much better if it is preceded by an introductory phrase:

- I was wondering how old the car is?
- Do you happen to know how old the car is?
- Do you think you could tell me how old the car is?
- Would you be able to tell me how old the car is?

to use twists with language recourir aux différentes nuances de la langue

bluntly franchement

Do you happen to know …? Sauriez-vous, par hasard, … ?

Checklist: sounding more polite

Check-list : paraître plus poli

This table summarises what you can say to sound more polite:

What you want to say / do	*What you say*
Win time, make your counterpart curious about what you are going to say or prepare them for disagreement	well actually right in fact to be honest
Give a negative statement	I'm afraid
Use a question instead of a statement to make it sound like a mere suggestion; a negative question sounds even more negotiable	Is Monday next week okay for you? Isn't Monday next week good for you?
Sound softer when refusing: 'would' instead of 'will'	That would be a problem.

What you want to say / do	*What you say*
Soften criticism – use words (qualifiers) such as 'very', 'slight', 'some', 'little', 'a bit', 'some'	This sounds like a slight problem. There are some reservations about the concept.
Make counter-suggestions using comparisons or negative questions	It may be more convenient to … Wouldn't Friday be better?
Use your voice for stress	Of course we *can* do this. This is quite a *large* sum.
Sound less pushy by using the continuous form	As I was telling you …
Avoid negative adjectives, even if they are linguistically correct	The idea doesn't seem to be very helpful. I'm not very happy with that.

mere simple
a sum une somme

pushy directif, insistant

A diplomatic game of give and take

Diplomatie et compromis

Discussion partners in English-speaking cultures are often more open to acknowledging their own mistakes if the other party is also willing to admit their share of responsibility for an error. The pattern that often emerges is an acknowledgement of responsibility followed by a polite request for one's discussion partner to do the same.

to be *(was, been)* willing to être disposé à

a share of responsability une part de responsabilité
a pattern un schéma, un modèle

Example: a little diplomacy goes a long way
Un peu de diplomatie peut mener très loin

A: As Robin said, we're unhappy with the quality of the goods you supplied and will be looking for you to make some kind of price reduction. I'm sure you can appreciate that we haven't been able to charge our customers full price for the goods.

B: I'm afraid that will be quite difficult for us at this late stage. We're prepared to take on board that some quality issues arose at the production stage. However, having carried out an internal investigation, we do feel that some of the features you point to were not adequately defined in the specifications you supplied to us. Would you be willing to concede that these points were not made clear to us from start?

A: With the benefit of hindsight, we can see that the specifications were not as clearly formulated as they should have been. But this doesn't change the fact that our tools division incurred substantial losses last year due to the substandard quality of the products you supplied.

B: Your business is very important to us, but unfortunately we just aren't in a position to offer a price reduction now that you have taken ownership of the goods. Could you perhaps see your way to considering a discount on your next order with us in lieu of a reduction?

A: That sounds like a workable solution. I'm sure it would go a long way towards soothing our Finance Director's headache.

B: Good. I'm very pleased to hear that.

to take *(took, taken)* on board that se faire à l'idée que
to carry out mener, réaliser
the features les caractéristiques
with the benefit of hindsight avec le recul
to incur losses subir des pertes
substandard quality de qualité inférieure
to take *(took, taken)* ownership of sth assumer la responsabilité de qqch
in lieu of à la place de
workable réalisable, raisonnable
to soothe calmer
a headache un mal de tête

Useful phrases

Acknowledging faults

Reconnaître ses erreurs

- We readily accept that some of the errors were due to a fault in our system ...
- I'm very sorry to say that we made a mistake with the order.
- As we've established, we need to address some serious issues in our production.

Asking for an acknowledgement

Les parts de responsabilité

- Could you perhaps see your way to accepting that there's also some room for improvement at your end?
- Would you be willing to accept / concede that there were also some issues at your end with regard to ...?

readily sans hésiter
an order une commande
to address sth s'occuper de qqch
some room de la place
at your end de votre côté

What to do in case of language problems

Que faire en cas d'incompréhension linguistique

There is far greater potential for misunderstandings when you are attending a meeting that is taking place in a foreign language. Perhaps you just didn't hear what a person said or their accent is difficult to understand. Or maybe differences in the ways people from other cultures express themselves can lead to confusion. It may also happen that your counterpart uses a word or expression you have never heard in your life.

Example: asking for repetition
Faire répéter

A: We are talking about one billion consumers in China.

B: Sorry, how many did you say? One million?

A: Oh, no. One billion, of course.

far greater bien plus grand
a foreign language une langue étrangère

one billion un milliard
how many combien

In any case, you should not hesitate to ask your counterpart for repetition and clarification – there's no shame in doing so. Just use the methods and phrases given on pp. 101-105 under *Enquiring and resolving misunderstandings*, namely

- asking for repetition,

- summarising for clarification,
- recapping and confirming.

there's no shame in … il n'y a pas de honte à…

Voting

Voter

Sometimes attendees cannot agree on an outcome. It may then be necessary to take a vote, which is usually done at formal meetings. However, voting should be seen as a last resort, as it will leave a number of attendees dissatisfied with the outcome. If a vote is necessary, the chair should keep strictly to the formal procedures.

A vote can either be done by secret ballot or by a show of hands. Before that, the subject of the voting has to be made clear. A suggestion or an idea that is to be put to a vote is called a 'motion'. Before a vote can be taken, a motion needs to be 'seconded', i.e. supported, by another person. When a motion is put to the vote and agreed on, you say that it is 'carried'. When there is no agreement, it is 'failed'. Usually, majority votes are taken. In case of a tie vote, the chairperson often has the deciding vote.

Of course, the outcome of the vote has to be recorded in the minutes, e.g. 'Motion to allow for flexitime, moved by Pierre' or 'Motion to allow for flexitime, seconded by Jeanne.'

Useful phrases

- Can I ask for a show of hands, please?
- All in favour? / All opposed?

- Those for / against the motion, please?
- Aye! [say 'aye' or raise your hand to show you agree]
- Any abstentions?
- The motion was carried unanimously.
- The motion has been rejected by four votes to two.

a ballot un scrutin
Carried! Adopté !
Failed! Rejeté !
a tie vote égalité des voix

flexitime des horaires souples
Those for / against, please? Qui est pour / contre, svp ?
Aye! Pour ! *(accepter)*

After the meeting

Après la réunion

Pour faire simple, la fin d'une réunion n'est que le début de la suivante. La plupart des réunions sont suivies de la rédaction d'un compte-rendu sur ce qui a été dit et convenu. Celui-ci doit alors être transmis aux participants.

Vous découvrirez, dans ce chapitre, comment :

- Réaliser le compte-rendu (page 118).
- Donner suite à la réunion et assurer les prochaines étapes (page 124).

Making the minutes
Réaliser le compte-rendu

The minutes have to be accurate and clear, summarising what was said. Lengthy sections can be boiled down to their essence. The minutes are usually circulated to all participants within a few days of the meeting and after approval by the chair. Remember that it is not necessary to include every word that is spoken, only important points and any votes and results. Indicating who said what is also necessary, which is why the minute-taker should make sure they know the names of the attendees. It is also recommendable to type out the minutes immediately after the meeting – this way you can make sure that you don't forget what was said.

lengthy très long
to boil down to se résumer à, revenir à
to type out saisir, rédiger

Examples

Example 1: short form for minutes
Compte-rendu : version courte

Minutes of the Steering Committee Meeting

Date: 1 February 2009, 7.00-8.40 p.m.

Venue: San Siro Meeting Room

Present: John Walsh, Bill Mc Kallen, Élise Duval, Sophie Leblanc, Thomas Denoyeau

Apologised: Anita Ferrarotti

1. New company brochure

There was positive feedback on the first revamped edition. There were 5,000 copies printed, more are needed next time. More photographs would enhance the overall appearance. Bill to contact PR for further action.

2. Decision-making process

In Greg's opinion, decisions taken by the steering committee were not valid unless the Project Leader and Management both agreed with the decisions. The other project members see this differently.

John pointed out that in all other departments the Project Leader was simply a project member with an allotted task.
Élise suggested the matter be clarified by a member of the board. The committee decided by four votes to one to have Dr Mc Kallen clarify the issue.
Sophie asked Greg what he was going to do about his position. He said he would think it over and submit his reply in writing.

3. AOB

Interest was shown in a new approach in marketing as briefly explained by John. To be followed up in the course of the next meetings. Thanks expressed to Sophie for doing an excellent job during the last trade fair in Paris.

Next meeting: To be announced.

Example 2: action minutes
Compte-rendu des actions

Minutes of the Steering Committee Meeting

Date: 1 February 2009, 7.00-8.40 p.m.

Venue: San Siro Meeting Room

Present: John Walsh, Bill Mc Kallen, Élise Duval, Sophie Leblanc, Thomas Denoyeau

Apologised: Anita Ferrarotti

1. Newsletter

BM reported that our newsletter was in high demand. However, he felt that it lacked conciseness and that a more modern look would be appreciated by the readers. The discussion ended with the general decision to look into the costs for a revamp.

Action: BM by 19 Feb.

2. Digital cameras

JW suggested our staff's mobile phones should be equipped with cameras to allow for faster transmission of on-site findings.

The committee members were not sure if this was necessary.

Action: All - decide by 20 Feb.

3. Floor plan - hot seating

ED proposed changing the seating arrangements, as not all staff are present in the office Mon-Fri.

SL added that the new home office day would also make for more desk space. Suggestion welcomed by committee members.

Action: ED design new floor plan by 19 Feb.

```
4. AOB
JW reported on his trip to Brazil. He made
substantial progress with the authorities and will
present the outcome at the next meeting.
Action: JW presentation 20 Feb.
TD reminded all to come up with ideas regarding
giveaways for the trade fair in Brussels in May.
Action: All by 20 Feb.
Meeting adjourned at 8.40 p.m.
Next meeting: February 20, 2009
Venue: San Siro
```

a venue un lieu
to revamp rafraîchir
to enhance mettre en valeur
PR (public relations) RP (relations publiques)
the steering committee le comité de direction
to allot attribuer
to think *(thought, thought)* sth over bien réfléchir à qqch
to lack manquer de
giveaways des cadeaux d'entreprise

Tips for minute-taking

Pour être un bon secrétaire de séance

Getting prepared

Ne pas négliger la préparation

If you work on a laptop computer, prepare a file containing the names of the participants and the items on the agenda. Then either take the laptop with you to fill in the key words during the discussion (to be formulated in full later on), or write them down on a sheet of paper and complete the minutes after the meeting.

Very often, initials are used to refer to participants who made a contribution or who are to carry out an action point. If you generally find it hard to remember people's names, make a habit of taking a brief note of their seating position during the introductions at the beginning of the meeting. It is best to write the names on a piece of scrap paper in the seating order. Use the attendance list to check if all the names are spelled correctly.

Writing style
Soigner sa plume

As a rule, the style is impersonal and concise. There are two ways of writing the minutes: one follows the chronological sequence of what was discussed, the other sticks to the written agenda (see examples, pp. 118-121).

It is a good idea to stick to the format, style and content of the minutes which were written for previous meetings. Every organisation has its own conventions.

to make *(made, made)* a habit of prendre l'habitude de

a scrap paper un morceau de papier

Les différentes manières de dire say
L'expression **he said** *(« il a dit ») devient lourde lorsqu'elle est répétée pour la troisième fois. Il faut donc essayer de varier les formulations en utilisant les verbes suivants :*
mentioned, **explained**, **confirmed**, **agreed**, **suggested**, **proposed**, **asked**, **introduced**, **discussed**, **reported**, **reminded**, **read out**, **indicated**, **pointed out**.

Checklist: the minutes

Check-list : le compte-rendu

In general, the minutes contain :
1 place and date of the meeting,
2 names of participants: present (also when they left, if they leave early) and absent,
3 subject of the meeting,
4 approval of the last minutes,
5 items on the agenda: discussions, outcomes, action items, who they are assigned to, deadlines,
6 any other business (AOB),
7 date, time and place of the next meeting.

Useful grammar

The minutes are generally written in the past tense. If reference is made to the future ('will' or 'going to') or the present, these tenses may also be used.

Another convention is to use the passive:

- No extra expense to be incurred without prior consent by the board.
- Session to be coordinated by John.

However, it is modern style to substitute as many unnecessary passives as possible with an active sentence structure. 'It was mentioned by John that …' sounds better if it is changed into an active sentence: 'John mentioned that …'

an approval une approbation
an expense une dépense

to incur engager
past tense le passé *(conjugaison)*

Following up the meeting

À la suite de la réunion

After the meeting, each role has its own duty to fulfil.

- The minute-taker has to get back to the attendees with the minutes in order to communicate the allotted tasks to the persons concerned.
- The chair has to follow up to ensure that all the agreed action items are carried out.
- The owners of action items should
  - complete them asap,
  - report back as agreed,
  - liaise with others, if necessary.

Example: email with attachment

E-mail comportant une pièce jointe

Subject: Minutes of the Steering Committee Meeting

Dear all,

I am writing to thank you all again for the fruitful meeting last Tuesday. Please find attached the minutes as well as the updated contact list.

Could you please get back to me asap regarding the time and date for the next meeting? John suggested the 20th at around 7.30 p.m. Please let me know if this is convenient.

I look forward to seeing you again soon.

Best regards,

Élise

to have *(had, had)* one's own duty to fulfil devoir remplir sa mission

asap *(as soon as possible)* au plus vite

to liaise with travailler en liaison avec

fruitful fructueux

to update mettre à jour

Special types of meetings

Les réunions spécifiques

Grâce aux technologies modernes, de nouveaux types de réunions, comme les vidéo-conférences, se sont rapidement développés. La gestion de projet et les techniques créatives ont aussi donné naissance à de nouvelles catégories de réunions. Les négociations et les réunions de clientèle accueillant de plus en plus de participants étrangers, il est devenu indispensable de prendre conscience des différences culturelles et de s'y adapter.

Ce chapitre vous aidera à appréhender les spécificités des :

- Réunions de clientèle (page 128) et négociations (page 132).
- Briefings et brainstormings (page 141).
- Réunions ordinaires et lancements (page 145).
- Téléconférences (page 148).

Meetings with customers
Les réunions de clientèle

Getting in touch
Prise de contact

Whether you meet the customer at their offices or at yours, make sure you make an appointment well in advance. Be prepared to offer several alternatives to suggest a meeting time that is really convenient for your (prospective) customer. Moreover, try to use the channel of communication that seems to be most appreciated by the other party: some people hardly ever check their emails, while others hate being disturbed by phone calls. But, first of all, you have to get in touch with them. When doing so, try to point out the specific issue that connects your company with them.

Useful phrases

- We used to have a branch office in Bruges, close to your headquarters in the city centre.
- I learned from your website that you also work with H&Z. We've been their preferred suppliers for eight years now.
- We did a similar project for ABC, Inc. three years ago.

a channel of communication un mode de communication
hardly ever presque jamais

headquarters le siège social
for eight years depuis huit ans
three years ago il y a trois ans

Identifying your client's needs

Identifier les besoins du client

Once you have managed to get an appointment for a meeting, what counts is responding to a client's needs. First you need to know what these needs are by finding out how your products or services meet the customer's requirements. If they don't meet them yet, think about how you could bring this about. Find examples among your references to show that you have already met similar needs in the past.

Useful phrases

- So you said you needed a new training partner for the Internet applications?
- When will you open the new plant in Hong Kong?

to bring *(brought, brought)* sth about provoquer qqch

among parmi
a plant une usine

Explaining your proposal in detail

Exposer votre projet en détail

Another crucial point is to create rapport with your customer, especially if this is a newly acquired customer. Apart from making small talk, you should establish common ground by telling them why your two companies fit together.

Useful phrases

- Did you see that our connector uses wireless technology?

- Can I draw your attention to the fact that fuel consumption is only three litres for this model?
- If you look at the illustration, you can see that this is where our product can be switched to 110 Volt. We use our own patent.

a newly acquiered customer un nouveau client
to fit ***(fit, fit)*** **together** se correspondre
wireless technology le réseau sans fil
to draw ***(drew, drawn)*** **one's attention** attirer l'attention de qqn
fuel consumption la consommation de carburant
to switch changer
a patent un brevet

Anticipating objections

Anticiper les objections

Any potential new customer will check out very carefully if you are the right person or company to meet its needs. Anticipate any concerns they may raise and address them by using positive statements.

Useful phrases

- We do have certificates according to ISO for the product.
- An export certificate is not required for shipments to Bali.
- You don't need to worry about different sockets, we build in the British version as standard.

to meet ***(met, met)*** **one's needs** répondre aux besoins de qqn
a shipment une cargaison
to worry about sth s'inquiéter de qqch
to build ***(built, built)*** construire

Ending the visit
Clore la visite

It is highly recommended that you save some time at the end of the meeting to address any questions. Even if you cannot give an answer off the cuff, you can make a list of action items to follow up by email or letter. And of course, don't forget to use friendly parting phrases to end on a positive note.

highly grandement
off the cuff au pied levé

parting phrases des phrases pour prendre congé

Useful phrases

- Are there any questions I could help you with?
- Could we perhaps discuss delivery periods next time? And then there is still the issue of transportation costs.
- Would next week suit you for another meeting?
- I'll email you the documents as soon as I can.
- It was a pleasure meeting you.
- Thank you for coming. It's been a fruitful meeting.
- Have a safe trip home!
- I'm looking forward to meeting you again next month.

Attentive hosts
Être un hôte attentif

Being an attentive host is most important in a customer meeting. Apart from small talk (see p. 52), this involves watchfulness and attention, e.g. by providing ice cubes for your American guests. Preparing an agenda for the meeting and making it available to the client beforehand will be appreciated and show that you really care about this sales contact, just as much as a thank-you letter after the visit, accompanied by the meeting minutes.

watchfulness la vigilance | **beforehand** à l'avance

Negotiations
Les négociations

Everybody negotiates. On a day-to-day level, just as when the stakes are high in an international merger, wage negotiations or for a customer-supplier contract. Apart from the principle of win-win, all sorts of tactics are employed deliberately. The most important thing, however, is to know what you want to walk away with. In general, the following tips apply to all types of negotiation:

Checklist: negotiations
Check-list : les négociations

1 Ask a lot of questions and listen, listen, listen. The more you find out, the better (See *Active listening*, p. 84).

2 Use diplomatic language whenever possible.

3 Make sure you are understood correctly.

4 Make it clear that you understand what the stakes are.

a stake un enjeu

a merger une fusion

wage negotiations des négociations salariales

the principle of win-win le principe gagnant-gagnant

to walk away with décrocher, remporter

Example: price negotiation

Négocier un prix

A: So, Will, how much do you have in mind, let's say per unit?

B: Well, it all depends on how many units you would like to sign up for on a regular basis.

A: Sure, but I would really need to hear a basic price from you first: I need to see if we are thinking along the same lines.

B: Okay, as you may remember from our written proposal we were thinking about 350 dollars per shipping unit.

A: 350 dollars! Are you kidding? I could get each pineapple wrapped in gold foil from the Ivory Coast at that price! And they would arrive in Europe much earlier, too!

B: But you know how the market is at the moment. Supply is at a premium. We have reserved 300 units for you because you are one of our long-standing customers. Otherwise we could have sold them already, and for a much higher price than that.

A: Okay, well, I will have to contact head office about that.

B: Certainly, there's no hurry, but don't forget our quality and reliability when it comes to delivery. Our fruit has always been good value for money.

A: I know, Will, I know. But what if the fruit goes bad during transit or if a container gets damaged? We would require insurance covering such events.

B: Of course we would grant you compensation, no question about that. The sum of the actual damage would have to be determined by an independent expert, however, at your expense.

A: If you don't mind, we'd better discuss this point next time. We can't move on this right now. And I feel quite tired after the long flight. I guess we should call it a day.

B: You're right. I want to see you in good shape tomorrow for the tour of the plantation.

A: So, before we meet next time, I'll find out about order quantities and you look into the point about shipping.

B: Right, and the insurance matter and the other outstanding issues as well.

A: Fine, so that's it then. Where are we going for dinner, Will?

to sign up s'engager

to think *(thought, thought)* along the same lines être sur la même longueur d'ondes

Are you kidding? Vous plaisantez ?

to be *(was, been)* at a premium valoir de l'or

good value for money un bon rapport qualité-prix

to grant sb sth accorder qqch à qqn

Établir un bon contact et prendre son temps

Au niveau international, il est important d'inviter ou d'envoyer la bonne personne à une négociation. Au Japon, un jeune manager ne sera pas accepté, même s'il bénéficie d'un pouvoir de décision. Il faut également tenir compte du fait que certaines cultures ont besoin de plus de temps pour prendre des décisions et attachent davantage d'importance, en premier lieu, à l'établissement d'une bonne relation. Certains ne feront affaire qu'avec une personne en qui ils ont confiance.

Useful phrases

Establishing common ground and reformulating

Trouver un terrain d'entente et reformuler les choses

- You know, the plot of land is worth a million right now.
- The track record of your module is really impressive.
- Let me check if I understood you correctly. You said you were looking for a long-term supplier?

a plot of land une parcelle de terre
the track record les résultats

Exploring positions

Analyser la situation

- Could I ask you how much you had in mind?
- When exactly do you need the material?
- Can you tell us what your standard terms are?

Making suggestions

Émettre des suggestions

- If you place an order for more than 5,000 units by the end of the month, we will ship them free of charge.
- We may agree to your terms, provided that you'll give us more leeway with regard to delivery times.
- It depends on how much you would be prepared to pay for our service.
- I'm afraid we can't accept that unless you offer us a three-year warranty.
- How about 50 pieces?
- Well, actually, 55 would be better.
- Why don't we try a more middle-of-the-road approach?
- Alternatively, we could offer you a discount.
- Let's think about preferred supplier status first.
- What if we offered you five per cent?

terms des conditions
a three-year warranty une garantie de trois ans

a middle-of-the-road approach une approche modérée

That might / may / would / could / can be an option!

Il est possible que...

Modal verbs are indispensable in negotiations. You can use them to vary the degree of certainty of your statements, i.e. you make what you say more or less probable.

- We *can* guarantee you delivery in five days. [Fact]

- We *could* deliver next week. [Real possibility]
- We *would* guarantee delivery ex works. [Possible, but under certain conditions]
- We *may* guarantee delivery to Marseilles. [Maybe]
- We *might* deliver to the Arab Emirates. [Faint possibility]

more or less plus ou moins
ex works en usine

a faint possibility une faible possibilité

Softening disagreement
Atténuer l'expression d'un désaccord

- I'm afraid we really can't agree to five per cent.
- Unfortunately, that's not really the way we see it.

Pushing for a decision
Pousser à prendre une décision

Soft-sell approach
De manière douce

- We would need to see some movement on price.

Hard-sell approach
De manière forte

- Take it or leave it!
- This is our final offer!
- We'll have to call the whole deal off / take our business elsewhere.

Take it or leave it! À prendre ou à laisser !

to call sth off annuler, abandonner qqch

Refusing

Refuser

Soft-sell approach

De manière douce

- I'm afraid that's not quite what we had in mind.
- I'm afraid this is as far as we can go.
- I am very sorry, but your offer still does not convince us.
- We feel that this is a bit much.
- I'm afraid I'm not in a position to grant you that.

Hard-sell approach

De manière forte

- No way! You know what the market is like right now.
- That's completely out of the question.

This is as far as we can go. Nous ne pouvons pas faire plus.

a bit much un peu trop

No way! C'est hors de question !

Asking for more time and looking ahead

Demander un temps de réflexion

- I'll have to think it over.
- I'll have to talk to my line manager about that.
- We can't give you a definite answer just now.
- As a next step we should look at …
- If you don't mind, I'd like to come back to that later.
- Let's not rush things.
- I don't think we should make a decision just yet.

Agreeing

Accepter

- That sounds / seems reasonable.
- That sounds like a sensible suggestion.
- In fact, that suits me fine.
- It's a deal!

a line manager un supérieur hiérarchique
a next step une prochaine étape
just yet tout de suite
It's a deal! Marché conclu !

Summarising what was agreed

Résumer ce qui a été convenu

- Can we run through what we've agreed?
- So, I'll summarise the important points of your offer.
- I'd like to check / confirm what we've said.

Next steps

Les étapes suivantes

- We need to meet again soon.
- So, the next step is to draft a formal contract.
- Before the next meeting we'll check the order quantities.

Le suivi
Un suivi écrit résume ce qui a été conclu et oblige l'autre partie à s'y résoudre. Cela montre également que vos intentions étaient louables. Parfois, une « lettre d'intention formelle » **(letter of intend)** *est envoyée avant toute signature de contrat.*

Useful grammar

How to express a must

Comment exprimer l'obligation

Don't forget that 'must' has no negative form and exists only in the present tense. 'Must not' means 'not allowed to' and, as it can only be used in the present tense, for all other tenses you have to resort to 'have to do sth' in its respective tenses:

- We *must* meet again to discuss the details.
- We *mustn't* forget to send the draft today.
- We *had to* organise the meeting differently.

If-clauses

Clauses introduites par if

An essential tool for bargaining are if-clauses. Particularly type I and II prove to be useful.

- Type I if-clause: The if-part of the sentence is in the present tense, the second part is formed by 'will' + infinitive. It is used to talk about real possibilities: 'If you agree on that, we will offer you a discount.'
- Type II if-clause: Type II is used to express a hypothetical possibility. The if-part of the sentence has to be in the past tense, with 'would' + infinitive in the second part: 'If you agreed on that, we would offer you a discount.'

All if-clauses can also be turned around, so that the if-clause forms the second part of the sentence, e.g. 'We *will offer* you a discount, if you *agree* on that.'

to bargain négocier, marchander

to be *(was, been)* turned around être inversé

Briefing and brainstorming

Briefing et brainstorming

What these two types of meetings have in common is that they require a subtle and careful facilitation style. In brainstorming sessions the chair should give the participants the opportunity to have their say and interrupt as little as possible; in briefings he or she should make sure all the information comes across.

Briefings

Les briefings

As the name suggests, a briefing should be kept short by definition. It should not take longer than 30 minutes. In a briefing the information has centre of attention. The idea is to share and spread knowledge. It is a one-way transfer of information from the organiser to the attendees. There is no exchange of ideas, nor are decisions taken. Questions may be asked by the persons being briefed.

to spread diffuser

a one-way transfer of information une diffusion d'informations

nor non plus

Example: briefing meeting for a facilitator
Réunion consacrée au briefing d'un modérateur

A: Thanks for coming in, Jeanne. Have you received the guidelines for the first group?

B: Yes, I have. In fact, I've read through them and I'd like to ask you some questions. As always, the devil is in the detail!

A: That's excellent, but first let me show you how the device works. Then I'd like to tell you what our main focus is.

B: Good, please go ahead. How do you switch it on?

A: The buttons are on the back panel, all of them.

B: I see. And what shall I say if people ask me who the sponsor of the study is?

A: Just tell them you don't know yourself, and that it is one of the major players in the market.

Useful phrases

- This is what we want to achieve: increased timeliness and accuracy.
- Just show your customers this list.
- There's no need to feel uneasy.
- Are these figures understandable?
- Do you understand what I am getting at?

The devil is in the detail! Le diable est dans les détails !
to go *(went, gone)* ahead continuer
the back panel le panneau arrière
a study une étude
timeliness la rapidité
accuracy l'exactitude
to feel *(felt, felt)* uneasy être inquiet
Do you understand what I am getting at? Vous comprenez où je veux en venir ?

Brainstorming sessions
Les séances de brainstorming

Brainstorming is a creative technique aiming at the maximum number of ideas to address a certain area of interest or to solve a problem. In the first step, the value or feasibility of the ideas generated is not an issue – all ideas are welcome. In general, brainstorming makes most sense for group sizes of 4 to about 20. Superiors or managers should only be invited if their subordinates will not feel inhibited by their presence. There should either be a time set for collecting ideas or a maximum number of ideas (50 to 100) fixed in advance. After that time, the ideas are categorised and sorted. But first of all, the topic of the brainstorming session has to be set out clearly. Furthermore, it is important that all participants make an active contribution. As a rule, criticising ideas is not allowed, as this might hinder inventiveness and spontaneity. It may sometimes be necessary for the chair or the facilitator to remind participants of these basic rules.

After the time set for collecting ideas is over or when there are no more ideas coming from the participants, the suggestions are sorted and categorised and any unfeasible ideas are deleted from the list. This can be done either as a group or by asking each person to pick out the five ideas he or she likes best.

to sort classer
to set *(set, set)* out formuler
to hinder entraver, freiner
to pick out choisir

Useful phrases

- So, how can we achieve better customer service?
- What aspects can enhance the overall customer experience?
- Can we agree not to interrupt each other?
- Can I ask you to save your comments for later, please?
- Let me remind you of the basic rules of brainstorming ...
- Can you please let Pierre finish what he was saying?

The following phrases may come in handy when taking notes on a flipchart during brainstorming.

- What was that again?
- Sorry, could you repeat / spell that for me, please?
- I think we have a double entry here.
- I see two main directions here, would you all agree?
- Can we filter out all the pros and cons, please?
- Shall we organise these ideas into two or three columns for a better overview?
- Can each of you now select the five ideas you think are the best?

to spell épeler
a double entry un doublon

the pros and cons les avantages et les inconvénients

Jours fixes and kick-offs

Réunions ordinaires et lancements

Jours fixes

Les réunions ordinaires

The term 'jour fixe' is derived from project management. The same day of the week and time is reserved for an internal meeting with the same people, e.g. the first Wednesday of a month or a week. The aim is to facilitate the exchange of information and to update all project members so they are at the same knowledge level.

to be *(was, been)* at the same knowledge level avoir le même nombre d'informations *(que les autres)*

Example: jour fixe team meeting

Réunion d'équipe hebdomadaire

A: … to put you all in the picture and bring you up to date with the latest developments.

B: Thank you, Nicolas. Are there any other points to be discussed?

C: Well, yes, actually, but it's a rather delicate issue.

B: Go ahead, Valérie, we're all curious.

C: Erm, right. It's about our colleague, Georges. He always passes the buck. He calls in sick every time a deadline is due.

A: I must say that I also find him very rude. [All the team nods]

B: I see, I see, so we seem to have an issue with Georges …

C: An issue! Are you kidding? I'm fed up with being on the same team, let alone in the same room with this guy.

B: Valérie, just try to take it a little easier on him.

C: Why are you defending him like that?

B: Well, I'm not supposed to tell you this, but Georges isn't too well at the moment. He was diagnosed with a serious illness and is currently undergoing treatment. This is why he is often away from work.

C: Oh, I'm so sorry, I had no idea!

A: That's a different story. Poor Georges!

to pass the buck se décharger de ses responsabilités
to call in sick se faire porter pâle
to be *(was, been)* rude être grossier
to be *(was, been)* fed up with en avoir assez de
Take it a little easier. Calmez-vous un peu.
I had no idea! Je ne savais pas !

Regular team meetings increase commitment and prevent misunderstandings and rumours. Apart from conveying information, it is important to foster the feeling of being appreciated among the team. This is why the participation of all team members should be encouraged. They should always be addressed by name, including when giving positive feedback: 'Thank you, Damien, for bringing this point up.'

to increase commitment renforcer les liens
to foster encourager, promouvoir

> ***Comment éviter l'ennui***
> *On peut varier les réunions en changeant la manière dont elles sont tenues, tout comme les activités qu'elles proposent. Il faut essayer d'encourager tous les participants à s'impliquer activement plutôt que de s'en tenir à une écoute passive.*

Kick-off meetings
Les réunions de lancement

Kick-off meetings are extremely important for the success of a new project. Their purpose is to signal to all team members and stakeholders that the project has now begun. They give the team orientation and direction and ensure that everyone understands what their roles are. As far as language is concerned, kick-off meetings contain the following features:

- introducing people (which is an important feature of a kick-off meeting, in particular when project owners and stakeholders have never worked together before),
- giving information (on the purpose of the project, its major deliverables, its risks and assumptions, as well as its milestones),
- getting agreement (on suggested project management procedures from all stakeholders),
- asking and answering questions.

a stakeholder un actionnaire
deliverables des éléments à fournir
an assumption une supposition
a milestone une étape importante

Telephone conferences
Les téléconférences

Telephone conferences (TCs) are increasingly widely used. Important factors for the success of a TC are a clear agenda, as well as the discipline of the participants and unambiguous communication. The agenda should contain the timing for individual points and the allocation of roles, such as the chair, timekeeper, secretary and the call facilitator, who takes care of the technical aspects.

a timekeeper un chronométreur

Agenda
L'ordre du jour

Example: subject of a telephone conference
Sujet d'une téléconférence

Agenda: outsourcing event organisation

Date: 5 May 2009, time: 11.00-12.00 CET

Participants: David Lejeune (chair), Peter Manson (call facilitator), Hélène Malavoi (timekeeper), Lisa Foster (secretary), Bridget Mayer, Sylvie Besançon, Benjamin Delcourt

Item	**Presented by**	**Time**
1. Apologies	DL	5
2. Minutes of the previous call	LF	5
3. Approval of agenda	DL	5
4. Report on London trade fair	SB	10
5. Outsourcing proposal - discussion	BM/all	25
6. Date for next conference call	DL	5
7. Feedback - discussion	DL	5

For a larger number of participants, it pays to prepare the agenda carefully and to circulate it in good time. The agenda should contain the timing for each point. When calculating the timing, you should bear in mind that each person's active contribution will take about three to five minutes per item. In our sample agenda, we have seven participants and 25 minutes allocated to the main discussion item. On the whole, the agenda should be kept as short as possible in order to limit the length of the meeting, as a TC is far more demanding in terms of concentration than a face to face meeting. If the TC is only held between a limited number of people and on a routine basis, an agenda is sometimes just made ad hoc, that is, at the beginning of the call.

Useful phrases

- Can we just quickly make a list of the items we need to talk about today?
- Does anyone have an agenda or do we need to jot a few items down so that we don't forget anything important?

a sample un modèle
on the whole dans l'ensemble

to make *(made, made)* sth ad hoc faire qqch de manière très précise
to jot sth down noter qqch

Starting a conference call

Débuter une téléconférence

Before the serious part of the conference call, participants are encouraged to make small talk, just as if they were meeting face to face. On the one hand, this will create better rapport between them, just as if they were in a real meeting. On the other hand, they can all tune in to each other's voices and accents – especially important for non-native speakers of English. Then, the chair starts the TC by welcoming the participants, doing a roll call, reviewing the agenda and summarising the aim of the TC.

Useful phrases

- Hi, this is Danielle. I'll be the chair in today's conference call.
- Can we go round the table and hear who has logged on already? Can you just say 'yes' when I call out your names?
- Before we start the ball rolling there are a few technical issues to clarify. Have you all received the agenda?
- Are there any other items we need to talk about today? Or any suggestions regarding the agenda?
- As you know, the main focus will be on the outsourcing business. It's important that we establish common ground on further procedure.

to tune in to être à l'écoute de
to do *(did, done)* a roll call faire l'appel
to log on se connecter
to start the ball rolling lancer la discussion

The chair should also clarify if participants need to leave the call early:

- Does anybody have to leave the call early?
- Yes, I do, actually. That's Pauline.
- Pauline, when do you have to log out?
- Around twelve at the latest.

By the same token, participants should announce if they are taking a break and let the others know when they are back in the TC:

- Sorry. It's Élise. I need to print out the agenda again. I'll be back in a minute.
- Anne here. I'm back in the call.

> ***Se présenter de façon efficace***
> *Si les participants ne se connaissent pas, ils doivent se présenter afin que les autres sachent qui ils sont et pourquoi ils rejoignent la téléconférence. Ils doivent préciser leur nom, comment ils veulent être appelés et en quoi consiste leur travail en faisant référence à un projet spécifique réalisé par le passé. Ils doivent également compléter leur présentation avec une phrase d'accroche plus personnelle afin de marquer les mémoires.*

Controlling the meeting
Animer la réunion

The chair has to involve all participants and ensure that they take turns. On the other hand, it is sometimes necessary to cut a speaker short. In any case, the role of timekeeper is vital for sticking to the agreed timings. He or she should remind everybody to keep it short. In longer TCs it sometimes makes sense to interrupt the call for a few minutes to give everybody a chance to collect their thoughts, to find some more information or simply to stretch their legs.

to take *(took, taken)* turns intervenir chacun son tour

to cut *(cut, cut)* s.o. short couper, interrompre qqn

to give *(gave, given)* sb a chance to do sth donner à qqn l'opportunité de faire qqch

to collect one's thoughts rassembler ses esprits

> ***Créer de bons rapports entre les participants***
> *Si vous voulez souligner le sentiment de groupe et mettre en place une atmosphère de coopération, vous devez utiliser le « nous »* **(the we-form)**. *L'usage du « nous » inclut chaque participant dans le groupe et favorise l'établissement de bons rapports*

entre les différents intervenants. C'est pourquoi il faut dire **We think this is a viable suggestion** *(« Nous pensons que cette suggestion est viable ») et non pas* **I think this is a viable suggestion** *(« Je pense que cette suggestion est viable »).*

Example: directing a TC

Mener une téléconférence

A: Bridget, would you kick us off, please?

B: Well, this is a great way to cut a lot of unnecessary spending. My figures show that we can save a lot of money.

C: Can I just come in here? That reminds me - we can't ask Marketing to organise the event again. It's unfair.

A: Sorry, Sonia, but I think this is a bit of a sidetrack. Let's try and keep to the agenda, okay?

C: Of course.

B: As I was saying, outsourcing the event organisation can really save a lot of money. It's obvious, if you ask me.

A: What do the others think? Is there anything else we should consider? Nothing? Okay. We seem to have dealt with the outsourcing issue. Let's move on to the website. We've budgeted 6,500 dollars to redesign it. Pierre, what do you think?

D: Well, obviously we need to make cuts and this would be less painful than many of the others. But we really have to prioritise PR because this is the bread and butter of our business. Perhaps we can consider a limited redesign?

C: I agree.

```
B: I do, too. You know, Pierre, speaking of
the website, you should really consider using a
different designer this time. I don't think the
last one did a good job at all.
```

to kick s.o. off commencer

to save money économiser de l'argent

It's unfair. C'est injuste.

It's obvious, if you ask me. C'est évident, si vous voulez mon avis.

to make *(made, made)* cuts procéder à des réductions

to be *(was, been)* painful être douloureux, faire mal

the bread and butter of l'essentiel de

Useful phrases

- Bridget, what do you think?
- Perhaps Marie could make a start with her opinion on item six?
- I need to hear your opinions about the new structure. Can we go round the group quickly? Fabien?
- Thank you, Sarah – Marc?
- Ludovic, I think Bridget wanted to add something? Go ahead, Bridget!
- Sorry, Toni, but I don't think this is really our topic today. Can I ask you to come back to the issue at hand?
- Sorry, Élise, but we said five minutes only for the review of the minutes.
- You've only got three minutes left, Marine. Could you speed your report up a little, please?
- Danielle, sorry to interrupt, just to remind you that we only have ten minutes left to wrap up the call.

- How about taking a ten-minute break here? Shall we reconvene at 12.45?

Documents are usually distributed by email before the TC. If you need to refer to them, you can use the following phrases:

- Could you all turn to page three, please?
- Have you all got a copy of the contract to hand?
- You'll find the total sum at the bottom of the page, on the right / in the bottom right-hand corner.

a ten-minute break une pause de dix minutes
to reconvene se réunir à nouveau

to hand sous la main
in the bottom right-hand corner en bas à droite

Ending a telephone conference
Mettre fin à une téléconférence

Wrapping up a TC involves the same elements as a normal meeting: summarising results, allocating action items and defining the next steps, including a time for the next meeting (see p. 72).

Useful phrases

- Let me sum up the arguments for and against outsourcing.
- If I understood right, most people were in favour of Bangalore as the location for our new subsidiary.

if I understood right ... si j'ai bien compris...
a subsidiary une filiale

Feedback on the TC

Remarques sur la téléconférence

If telephone conferences are held on a regular basis, it is useful to ask the participants for their feedback on how the TC worked for them. The results can then be discussed at the beginning of the subsequent meeting or beforehand by email. Improving how TCs are run will ensure their ongoing success. The feedback should cover the following questions:

- Did the technical equipment work well?
- Were the timings adhered to?
- What could be done better?
- What should we continue to do and what should we stop doing?
- What should be avoided?

to hold *(held, held)* tenir
to improve améliorer
ongoing en cours

Checklist: TC dos and don'ts

Check-list : les choses à faire et à ne pas faire lors d'une téléconférence

1	Introduce yourself the first time you speak: 'Hello, everyone. My name is … and I work in the … department.'
2	Make small talk to give the other participants a chance to 'tune in' to your voice and way of speaking: 'How is the weather over in California? It's rainy here in Lyons.'
3	When introducing yourself, mention something personal plus a memory hook so that the others will remember you better.

4 Speak slowly, clearly and concisely. Use your voice actively, as people cannot see your facial expression.

5 Use your name every time: 'This is John speaking …'

6 Describe your body language, for example: 'I'm shaking / nodding my head here.'

7 Announce that you are leaving or returning after a break, for example: 'This is John speaking, I am about to leave the call for five minutes. / This is John, I'm now back in the call.'

8 Keep in mind that all paper rustling, sipping or clicking pens will be heard by everybody.

9 If you ask somebody for their input, address them with their name, repeating the question if necessary.

10 Learn how to work the equipment properly, especially the mute button: remember others might hear the hold music while it is pressed.

11 Don't sit on a leather chair! The sounds it makes when you move around will be quite startling to yourself and others. A fabric-covered chair is much safer.

a memory hook un aide-mémoire

to be *(was, been)* about to do sth être sur le point de faire qqch

a paper rustling un froissement de papier

the mute button la touche sourdine

a leather / fabric-covered chair une chaise en cuir / en tissu

Literature

- *How to manage meetings*, Alan Barker, Kogan Page, London, 2002
- *The language of meetings*, Malcolm Goodale, LTP, Hove, 1987
- *Fifty ways to improve your Telephoning and Teleconferencing Skills*, Ken Taylor, Summertown Publishing, Oxford, 2008

Index

active listening 84
agenda 19
– introducing the 63
– keeping to the 68
– telephone conference 148
agreeing 87, 139
apologies 61
asking for more information 82
asking for repetition 102
booking facilities 34
brainstorming 141
briefing 141
bringing the meeting to a close 74
cancelling 17
clarification 104
conditional tense 14
confirming 17, 105
consensus 70
criticism 95
dates 11
dealing with participants 65
decision 137
disagreement 89, 137
encouraging participants 66
evening entertainment 40
explaining your proposal 129
getting in touch 128
hierarchies 39
if-clauses 140
information on local accommodation 29
initiating further action 72
initiating the discussion 63
interrupting 81
introducing oneself and others 49
jours fixes 145
kick-off meetings 147
lift talk 46
lunch meetings 12
minutes 118
negotiations 132
objectives 63
opinion 99
polite questions 108
recapping 105
receiving visitors 44
refusing 138
requirements 30
rescheduling 14
responding 10, 85
roles 78
seating arrangements 39
small talk 52
submitting items 24
suggestions 8, 98, 136
summarising 69, 139
telephone conferences 148
thanking the attendees 76
times 11, 36
travel directions 28
voting 114
weather 27

Blay Foldex/Berlitz
40-48, rue des Meuniers
93108 Montreuil Cedex
France
Téléphone : 01 49 88 92 10
Fax : 01 49 88 92 09
info@berlitzeditions.fr

HAUFE.

Lisa Förster, Annette Joyce, *Meetings in English*

Licensed edition by the Haufe-Lexware GmbH & Co. KG, Federal Republic of Germany, Freiburg, 2010
Lizenzausgabe der Haufe-Lexware GmbH & Co. KG, Bundesrepublik Deutschland, Freiburg 2010

1re impression septembre 2010 / Imprimé en France.

Coordination version française : Vanessa Redureau